Experiencing Lithuania
An Unconventional Travel Guide

COLUMBIA J. WARREN

The website addresses provided throughout this book are offered as
resources to readers. Inclusion of a website is not in any way intended to be or to imply an endorsement of the website or its content.

Cover design by Arnas Palubinskis; cover photograph of a stork (the
national bird of Lithuania) by Kazys Mikalauskas. Other photograph
credits are located in the Photo Credits appendix.

Information is available at www.experiencinglithuania.com.

For Jūratė

CONTENTS

ACKNOWLEDGMENTS

First and foremost, I would like to thank my wonderful wife, Jūratė, for introducing me to Lithuania, for her significant encouragement, and for her tremendous assistance with completing this guide. This has truly been a collaborative effort. Without her, this guide would not have been possible, and I never would have had the pleasure of getting to know Lithuania.

Special thanks to the many Lithuanians who have been so hospitable during my visits: Lina and Mindaugas; Ramutis and Vanda; Jonas and Aldona and their family; Sandra; Laura; and many others.

Thanks to the people who graciously provided lists of their favorite restaurants and other recommendations: Lina and Mindaugas; Sandra; Agnė and Mantas; Eglė; Viktorija and Tadas; and Audra.

Thank you to everyone who has reviewed this work: Sarah; Rūta; Amy and Fred; my mother, Kate; and Aušra.

I would also like to thank everyone who has given permission to use their photography in this book, especially Kazys Mikalauskas for generously allowing the use of his gorgeous aerial photographs, including the cover photo.

Preface

Lithuania is a wonderful country that I love to visit, and I am eager to share my enthusiam and knowledge with readers of this guide. I have enjoyed the process of learning about Lithuania and Lithuanians with the help of my wife, which in turn has greatly enhanced my experiences in Lithuania. I hope that the information I provide in this book will enhance your experiences as well.

This guide takes a different approach than other more traditional travel guides about Lithuania. Instead of superficial aggregation of information about the country and its tourist attractions, I try to delve deeper into describing the country and its people, particularly those aspects about Lithuania and Lithuanians that strike me as different, unique and interesting. I do provide descriptions about places to go, sites to see, and where to eat, but only selectively based on my own and local Lithuanians' recommendations. I also provide a great deal of advice about traveling in Lithuania in order to help you make the most of your visit.

Experiencing and pondering the differences between our own country and the countries we visit allows us an opportunity to play armchair sociologist, anthropologist, economist, legal analyst, or political scientist. In Lithuania, you have a people who are a part of modern Europe, but still celebrate and are very proud of their heritage; a people most of whom are Catholic, but revel in nature and their pagan history; a people who are embracing democracy and a free market economy, but retain some entrenched sensibilities from Soviet times. All of these characteristics and many more affect who Lithuanians are, how they think, how society operates, and how they interact with outsiders.

There are many intriguing aspects of Lithuania to discover as you travel the country. You may find yourself asking "What the heck is this on my plate?" "Who stole my shower curtain?" "Is that guy drunk or just Estonian?"[1] While there is much that will be familiar in Lithuania, there are also plenty of interesting differences that you will come across.

This guide is, of course, heavily dependent on my own experiences in Lithuania, so it will focus on some aspects of the country while forsaking others that are no less worthy of description. For instance, I know very little about some of the major cities, including Šiauliai and Panevėžys, so I have not provided information about them. I have also written extensively about the resort town of Druskininkai, exhibiting my affinity for this town that is perhaps out of proportion with its size.

This guide is written from my perspective as an American, but the vast majority of my commentary will resonate with anyone from outside of Lithuania. Of course, as a foreigner, I will surely make errors, so please excuse any mistakes. I would also note that Lithuania is a dynamic and fast-moving country, and what is true today may no longer be accurate tomorrow. The pace of change is really quite astonishing.

This guide is divided into four main parts. In Part I, I give an overview of Lithuania and its people. In Part II, I describe recommended places to visit, dine and recreate. In Part III, I pro-

---

[1] The answers are: 1. probably something from a potato or a pig; 2. trolls; and 3. likely both.

vide practical advice about a wide range of logistical matters. Finally, in Part IV, I present a concise history of Lithuania. These parts can certainly be read in any order you prefer.

Note that I have not included maps in this guide, but have instead included detailed maps on the guide's website at www.experiencinglithuania.com.

I hope you enjoy the following meandering tour through Lithuania.

Part I

About Lithuania

The Basics

Knowledge about Lithuania (or **Lietuva** in Lithuanian) among North Americans seems to generally be comprised of one or more of the following three facts: (1) Lithuania was the first country to declare independence from the USSR (which it did on March 11, 1990); (2) the capital of Lithuania is Vilnius; and (3) the 1992 Olympic basketball team, sponsored by the Grateful Dead, wore tie-dyed jerseys (they won the bronze medal; bonus points if you knew this before the release of "The Other Dream Team" documentary). Don't worry if you scored 0/3 of the facts above – after reading the next few pages, you will know more about Lithuania than 99.999% of Americans. Congratulations!

The first fact that most Lithuanians would like foreigners to know is that they are not Russians, nor are they Slavic. This is a common misperception that is especially painful for Lithuanians because Russians have been occupiers of the country for most of the last two centuries.

Lithuania is situated in Northeastern Europe, with borders along the Baltic Sea, the Russian exclave of Kaliningrad, Poland, Belarus and Latvia. Lithuania, Latvia, and Estonia are often referred to as the "Baltics" or the "Baltic states." (These should not to be confused with the Balkans in Southeastern Europe, which include the countries of the former Yugoslavia, among others.) The country is roughly the same size as West Virginia. Most of Lithuania falls between the 54th and 56th parallels, approximately the same as Newfoundland (as a reference, New York City is around the 41st); however, the temperatures are moderated somewhat by favorable ocean currents. Nonetheless, Lithuania is relatively cold, with temperatures rarely reaching the 80°s F (27° C) in the summer and regularly falling below 0° F (-18° C) in the winter. Anecdotally, though, it does seem as though summer temperatures have been on the rise in recent years.

Maps of Lithuania

If you have a choice of when to travel to Lithuania, I would highly advise going sometime in May through September when it's warmer and the days are longer. On the other hand, there is something quite special about visiting in the winter, as it can be great fun to take saunas or gather together inside after a cold walkabout. Being chilly may actually be a quintessential Lithuanian experience that you should have at some point! If you come in late spring or early summer, many cities and towns have "town days" that include musical performances and vendors. Whenever you come, prepare for the possibility of cold weather and precipitation.

The population of Lithuania is approximately 3.25 million, comprised of about 84% ethnic Lithuanians, 6.1% ethnic Poles, 4.9% ethnic Russians, 1.1% ethnic Belarusians and 3.9% other ethnicities and nationalities. The proportion of ethnic Russians in Lithuania is significantly lower than in Estonia (25.6%) and Latvia (27.8%), resulting in a much less tumultuous integration of the Russian population, and less hostility from Russia, as compared to those countries. Lithuania is experiencing fairly significant population decline, with a population loss of approximately 8% since 2000 and 12% since 1990.

The religion of most ethnic Lithuanians is Roman Catholic, unlike the Protestant Latvians and Estonians, reflecting their very different histories.

The flag of Lithuania is a horizontal tricolor of yellow, green and red. Reflecting its tropical climate, abundance of savannah wildlife, and frequent dengue fever outbreaks, Lithuania shares these colors with many African countries such as Cameroon, Ethiopia, the Congo, Ghana, Mali, Senegal, and Guinea. (Okay, there doesn't actually seem to be any logical connection – this appears to just be a strange coincidence of history.)

The coat of arms of Lithuania is the Vytis ("Chaser") – an image of a knight on horseback wielding a shield with a cross with two bars (this cross is the symbol of the Jagiellonian dynasty). The Pillars of the Gediminids (sometimes called Pillars of Gediminas) also symbolizes Lithuania and more specifically the Gediminid dynasty.

Throughout this guide I have quoted prices in the local currency, the **litas** (LTL). The exchange rate tends to be around 2.5LTL/1USD (and is pegged at 3.45LTL/1EUR). A more detailed discussion about money is provided in the Money and Buyin' Stuff section. Note also that I have generally provided adult admission prices; discounted prices for children, students, and seniors are usually available.

There is a great deal of useful information about traveling to Lithuania at the official tourism website at www.lietuva.lt/en.

Lithuania and Lithuanians

Although Lithuania is a relatively small country, there is nonetheless extraordinary variation among its people and places. It is a beautiful country, but retains some scars from its difficult past. The built environment of Vilnius and other Lithuanian cities is representative of that past, which has been very much a rollercoaster of triumphs and tragedy. To put it mildly, Lithuania has experienced significant turmoil throughout the recent centuries. I think an understanding of the country's past is very important to appreciating what you will see and experience on a visit. For that reason, I highly recommend that you read the history of Lithuania in Part IV (a whirlwind tour through the country's history in a few short pages – what a deal!).

It is, of course, impossible to adequately describe a people and place in just a few pages, but I will do my best to provide a decent overview. I encourage you to travel to Lithuania and experience it for yourself. I hope that you will have the opportunity to meet Lithuanians on more than a superficial level and see enough of the country that you come to some understanding of the rich beauty it possesses. If you are not visiting friends or relatives, I highly recommend that you engage the services of a local guide in some of the places you visit to help you in fully experiencing Lithuania.

Despite years of war and Soviet occupation, the cities of Lithuania, especially Vilnius, retain impressive historical structures. The old town of Vilnius is the largest old town in Eastern Europe and has many beautiful Baroque buildings. Kaunas and

Klaipėda also have great old towns. The country now also exhibits quite a few examples of rather unattractive Soviet architecture, in particular the ubiquitous yellow or red brick apartment buildings. These buildings certainly provide an interesting glimpse into a period of time when aesthetics (and quality) were low on the list of priorities.

View of Vilnius Cathedral and Gedimino prospektas

Although there are many amazing sites in Lithuania, visitors should have realistic expectations about what they will see. Many of the structures of Lithuania may appear quite modest compared to some cities in Western Europe. There aren't any individual sites that will blow you away – there is no Notre Dame Cathedral, no Taj Mahal, no Machu Picchu, no Pyramids of Giza. Instead, I think the beauty and history of the country will grow on you in time as you explore. I think there is a great benefit to this, as you are freed to contemplate what you are *experiencing* in Lithuania, not just focus on what you are *seeing*.

Forest trail in a birch and pine forest near Trakai

Outside of the cities, Lithuania boasts beautiful natural land-scapes. As much as Vilnius and other Lithuanian cities are the hubs of activity, in my mind it is the rural areas that are the true attractions of the country. Pine and birch forests stretch over a large part of the country and small lakes dot the landscape. Multiple rivers wind lazily through the gentle contours of the countryside. Wetlands with a wide range of wildlife abound as a result of the generally flat and low-lying landscape. Farmlands also cover large plots of land in the rural areas. The "highlands" of the northeastern part of the country contain rolling hills and plenty of lakes.[2] In addition, the country has some gorgeous coastline, especially along the famous Curonian Spit, a sand dune covered peninsula stretching about 60 miles along the coast (the northern part of which is in Lithuania, while the southern part is in Kaliningrad). One of the greatest attractions of the country is the vast areas of relatively unspoiled nature.

---

[2] In a land with rather modest topographical characteristics, Lithuanians seem to have a warped sense of scale – they call a hill a "mountain" (**kalnas**) and actually have a name for something smaller than a "mountain" (**kalva**).

As with most countries, Lithuanian society is multi-layered and complex, so any generalizations to be made about Lithuanians will of course not apply to everyone. With that said, following are some sweeping generalizations for you to consider!

As a foreigner arriving in Lithuania, you might get a first impression that Lithuanians are unhappy because they tend to not smile very much, instead exhibiting a particular fondness for frowning. Lithuanians aren't necessarily unhappy, but they don't generally display outward signs of emotion to strangers. As I have been told, if you smile at someone random on the street, they will likely think that you are mentally challenged (I think this is akin to being seen as a "grinning idiot"). While this may be the case for the older generations, you could say that Lithuania is "defrosting" a bit, as younger Lithuanians generally do not come across as quite as cold to strangers, and you might even see some random smiles among them.

The frowning and outward appearance of seriousness among Lithuanians reflects a national characteristic embodied in the concept of a "**rimtas žmogus**" which is roughly translatable as a "serious person". The qualities of a rimtas žmogus are a sort of ideal character type for Lithuanians – seriousness, discretion, reliability, stoicism, trustworthiness, etc. As Lithuania has traditionally been a fairly hard place to live, these qualities were valued highly, and much of that national character continues today even as such Western frivolity as Will Farrell movies and Lady Gaga entice the younger generations.

I think one of the most fascinating aspects about Lithuanians and their culture is their resiliency. Lithuania is extremely fortunate to even exist at all, given its precarious position in Europe and its history of conflict with generally much more powerful neighbors. In fact, prior to its current period of independence since 1990 and a short period of independence during 1918 to 1939, Lithuania had not been a truly independent country since 1385 (though it was fairly autonomous between 1385 and 1569). Many other peoples in similar situations, such as Old Prussians[3], have been assimilated into other groups and ceased to exist, but Lithuanians remain.

It is also interesting to consider the present circumstances of Lithuania in terms of how territorial boundaries are established and accepted. As is described more fully in the History of Lithuania section, there are many events that have shaped the country's current borders. Many times in modern history, the larger geopolitical situation has played a dominant role, whereas the legitimacy or illegitimacy of territorial claims has been secondary.

As a small country, Lithuania shares some interesting characteristics with other small countries and even small U.S. states. First, Lithuanians quite often take great pride in anything or anyone successful or famous from the country, whether or not related to that person's local area. In a sense, everything in Lithuania is local. I have also noticed this phenomenon in smaller, less-populated U.S. states, like Vermont. Second, the threshold for being famous in Lithuania is rather low, resulting in what I have termed being "Lithuania Famous". I've been amazed at who is deemed a "star" for the purposes of Dancing with the Stars type shows.

Lithuanians are tremendously hospitable if you are fortunate enough to be invited into their inner circle as a guest. I have

[3] Not to be confused with the Germanic people who took over the area and came to be known as Prussians.

had the great privilege of being welcomed into the homes of quite a few Lithuanians, and I have never left hungry or thirsty! You will likely hear a lot of **"Prašom valgyti!"** (Please eat!) during your stay. And eat you should. My best memories of visits to Lithuania have come from the gatherings of family and friends around a table.

One other generalization that seems applicable to a wide swath of the population is that Lithuanians tend to really love nature – to get out into the forests, walk in parks, swim in lakes, and generally spend time outside. This may be a trait shared by a lot of Northern Europeans who seek to enjoy the precious short periods of the year when being outside is tolerable.

Somewhat related to Lithuanians' interest in nature is their pride in the nation's pagan history. Prior to Christianization, Lithuanians worshipped a pantheon of gods and goddesses, similar to Norse/Greek/Roman deities, and the natural world played a central role in the religion. In addition to its connection with nature, paganism is also closely connected with the unification, growth and strength of the early Lithuanian nation. During the 10th through 14th centuries, Lithuania constantly repelled invaders who were ostensibly attempting to convert the Lithuanians from paganism to Christianity, but more importantly had ambitions on Lithuania's territory. Although today Lithuania is Catholic[4], it retains quite a few vestiges of pagan times, such as people's names, holidays, superstitions, decorations, and other traditions. It should be noted that "paganism" in Lithuania and Northern Europe has a very different conno-

---

[4] Leaders of Lithuania eventually voluntarily Christianized the country, partly because they realized there was significant advantage in taking paganism away as an excuse for the territorial ambitions of their aggressive Christian neighbors. The Pope would no longer endorse "crusades" against Lithuania once it was Christianized.

15

tation than it does in the U.S. and some other parts of the Western world. It is a common part of the culture and traditions, and is not viewed as a wacky, outside-the-mainstream ideology, but rather it has some romantic, getting back to nature connotations. In fact, a renaissance of some pagan traditions related to nature seems to be in vogue in Lithuania.

Lithuanians also seem nostalgic for, and proud of, their agricultural roots. Most Lithuanians are only a generation or two removed, if at all, from a rural agricultural lifestyle. The Lithuanian economy (ethnic Lithuanians in particular) was heavily dependent on agriculture well into the mid-twentieth century. Traditional farming was centered around the small farm homestead (**sodyba**). During Soviet times, city dwellers stayed connected with the land due to the small-scale farming performed at each family's **sodas** (garden plot, like the Russian *dacha*) situated near the cities.

Traditional sodybos in rural Lithuania

Many urban Lithuanians today enjoy visiting the countryside, and agritourism is becoming quite popular. It is also fairly common for urban residents to buy and renovate sodybos in the countryside to use as places to visit on the weekends or during vacations. Traditional Lithuanian cuisine, consisting of simple, hearty foods, is still fairly popular, even among the young urban population.

While revering the past and traditions, younger Lithuanians are certainly well-integrated into international culture. Music, clothes, and other products from abroad are prevalent. Urban residents, especially those in Vilnius, are as cosmopolitan and sophisticated as any in Western Europe. In many ways, Lithuania has caught up to the West quickly since the restoration of independence.

Lithuania is facing some difficulties, though, that bear noting because they provide some context for outsiders visiting the country. Of course, I recognize that every country has its problems – the U.S. certainly has its fair share as well! Economic problems are evident in the country, both because of the recent economic crisis (**krizė**) and also because the transition from communism to capitalism left many in the older generations out in the cold (both literally and figuratively). The country is also struggling with issues of tolerance, especially related to the rights of minority populations, and with racism and homophobia. Interestingly, gender equality is fairly good – one of the few positive legacies of the communist past. On a completely different plane due to the historical context, anti-Semitism also remains a significant issue in the country. Lithuania seems to be struggling somewhat with integration into a Europe that to a certain extent came to terms with various social issues during the twentieth century, while the Soviet Union kept such issues under wraps. Like many countries in Europe, Lithuania is also experiencing a resurgence in nationalism and there appears to be some public debate about what it means to be a unique nation within the larger European and global context.[5]

I would also note my sense that Lithuanians harbor somewhat mixed emotions about Western Europeans and North Americans. Without a doubt, most Lithuanians are friendly, inviting, and genuinely interested in meeting visitors. I get the sense, however, that the average Lithuanian's positive view of Western Europeans and North Americans is mixed with some slight feelings of envy and bitterness, especially for Americans. It is important to know that Lithuanians carried significant expectations that the West would assist them in their fight for liberation from the USSR in the period following WWII. In the end, this did not occur and Lithuanians were left on the wrong side of the iron curtain.[6] As my wife's father has remarked, "The war did not end for Lithuania in 1945." I think there is some lingering resentment over this abandonment and the ensuing deprivations, juxtaposed with the relative wealth and advancement of Western European and North American countries. This is exacerbated by the fact that the West has focused significant attention on the Holocaust, while nearly ignoring the perhaps equally terrible atrocities committed by Stalin.

---

[5] Without intending to excuse the evils that can arise in the name of "nationalism," it is worth considering how a small nation such as Lithuania even exists today after so many periods of occupation, oppression, and attempts to extinguish it as a nation. While often viewed negatively, nationalism is at its core a process of defining and protecting the unique characteristics – traditions, language, ethnicity, etc. – that define that nation, often in the face of attempts to destroy them.

[6] It's also worth noting that the lack of American support for Lithuania goes back even to the period following WWI. The U.S. advocated that the territory of the pre-war Russian Empire should be returned to Russia's control.

It is interesting to note that, perhaps partly based on the experience of being abandoned in the face of Russian hostilities, Lithuanians have a strong connection with the country of Georgia. Although the current government has taken a slightly more conciliatory stance toward Russia, the Lithuanian government has a history of advocating for Georgia. The two countries maintain fairly close ties, and Lithuanian activists are quite a bit more involved with supporting Georgia than one would otherwise expect based on their geographic and cultural differences.

Today, Lithuania is emerging out of a very dark period with a bright future. With no mal-intent, I think one of the most exciting aspects of the country is its tremendous potential. In just the half decade that I have been visiting the country, I have seen so many changes and so much modernization. In the two decades since the restoration of independence, the country has changed to an almost unbelievable extent. I can feel the excitement that many Lithuanians have about the prosperity accruing to their country. It really is a new era for Lithuania, and I know that Lithuanians are eager to invite you to their country and share it with you.

Regions of Lithuania

Lithuania is comprised of four (or five) "ethnographic" regions: Suvalkija, Aukštaitija, Dzūkija, and Žemaitija, and some consider Lithuania Minor a fifth region. These regions are not official administrative units, but rather represent historical and cultural regions.

Aukštaitija is the largest region and is located in the central and northeastern part of Lithuania. The name of the region literally means "highlands," owing to the slightly higher elevation of the area (relative to the rest of Lithuania and the surrounding countries). The region boasts the Aukštaitija National Park, with many beautiful lakes and hills. This region was the heart of Medieval Lithuania and the place from which Lithuania's power emanated.

Bend of the Nemunas river in Dzūkija

Dzūkija is the region that stretches across southern Lithuania and into Belarus and Poland. The region is heavily forested with fairly infertile soil, and is known for the mushrooms and berries that grow prolifically throughout those forests. Dzūkija National Park is a beautiful and pristine area to visit. During the summer and autumn, there are often many people out beside the roads selling mushrooms and berries. A well-known saying about Dzūkija is "If not for mushrooms and berries, Dzūkian girls would be naked" (**"Jei ne grybai ir ne uogos, dzūkų mergos būtų nuogos"**), to which I've received the wise-ass response "They dress Dzūkian girls in mushrooms and berries?"

Suvalkija (formerly known as Užnemunė) is a small region in the southwestern part of the country that stretches into Poland, and is named for the town of Suwalki that is today located in Poland. Suvalkija is considered relatively new as a distinct region in Lithuania, as it was all part of Poland until 1920, although many ethnic Lithuanians have lived in the region since the 15th century. Suvalkija was a very important region in the emergence of the Lithuanian national movement that led to the establishment of an independent Lithuania in 1918.

Žemaitija (also known as Samogitia) is located in the northern part of Lithuania, and has a history that is the most distinct from the other ethnographic regions. The region was, at various times during its history, an independent entity, part of Livonia (present-day Latvia under the control of the Teutonic Knights and other German groups), and integrated within Lithuania. To this day, many Žemaitijans consider themselves somewhat separate from the rest of Lithuania and the region's dialect is fairly different from those spoken in the other regions.

The fifth region, Lithuania Minor, is the area containing ethnic Lithuanians that spans the coast of Lithuania and into Kaliningrad. This region was outside of Lithuanian territory for most of history, and was only incorporated into Lithuania in the 20th century. Lithuania Minor includes Klaipėda, the major port city of the country, as well as the Curonian Spit. The region also includes the Nemunas Delta Regional Park, a very important wetlands area with massive populations of migratory birds.

Nature

Lithuania is covered with many forests and marshes, and has beautiful rivers and lakes, providing great opportunities to enjoy the natural environment. Lithuanians generally love to be outside in nature and often use the phrase "**važiuojam į gamtą**" ("let's go to nature") to describe their weekend plans for visiting the country's natural areas.

Many urban Lithuanians have relatives who live out in the rural areas or have access to their family's **sodas**. **Sodai** are an interesting phenomenon that has evolved significantly since Soviet times, when each family was allocated a small sodas (garden plot) of generally about 6 ares (approximately 6,450 sq. feet or 0.15 acres). Families were permitted to grow their own fruits and vegetables for personal use or to barter. These sodai were one of the few avenues for entrepreneurship in Lithuania, and were actually incredibly productive, yielding a sizable portion of the fruits, berries and vegetables consumed by a family. It was permitted to erect a structure on the land, but it could not have heating and had restrictions on size. Since independence, these restrictions have been lifted, and many of the structures have been converted and expanded into fully functional residences. These residences, used as country cottages, second homes, or even primary residences, allow many Lithuanians to spend time out in natural areas.

For those who do not have access to a sodas or to a relative's house in the country, or for those who want to explore other areas, agritourism is becoming a popular way to visit the countryside. Guests are able to stay at a sodyba and enjoy the beautiful rural areas of Lithuania. I have spent many great days and nights at a beautiful lakeside cottage near Druskininkai run by close relatives of my wife (www.en.samanis.lt). You can find other agritourism cottages throughout Lithuania on the website www.countryside.lt.

Agritourism cottage at Samanis

When out in the rural areas of Lithuania, you will certainly see many aspects of an older way of life. There are plenty of smaller farming plots throughout the countryside. If you are visiting in the summer, many fields will be aglow with the yellow flowers of rapeseed (also known as canola), a common crop in Lithuania. You might also notice single cows out grazing in fields near the road. Some rural families in Lithuania still have the "family cow" that is set out to graze, attached by rope to a stake in the ground. It's also common to see horse-drawn carts being driven on rural roads.

Another thing in rural Lithuania that I find amusing is bus stops that appear to be absolutely in the middle of nowhere – with people waiting at them! Apparently there are actually small villages somewhere within a few miles, but it is such an odd sight to see.

One of the most enjoyable activities out in nature, particularly in the Dzūkija region of southern Lithuania, is mushroom picking. This can have the feel of a treasure hunt, and can really be quite addictive. Mushroom picking is most often conducted rather early in the morning, so as to beat the other mushroom hunters to the mushrooms that emerged overnight. Lithuanians don't share the locations of their secret spots with just anyone, so try to buddy up with someone who can show you the way. Even I now have my own secret spot deep in the forest near Druskininkai.

Of course, if you're American or Canadian, you aren't likely to go searching for mushrooms on your own anyway since we've all been trained to be deathly afraid of picking wild mushrooms. Have no fear if you are out with a Lithuanian guide; they are well acquainted with the types of mushrooms to pick. If you want to go searching, I recommend trying one of the many dirt roads leading off the A4 in the Dzūkijos nacionalinis parkas near Druskininkai.

The two types of mushrooms most commonly sought in Lithuania are the chanterelle (**voveraitė**), which generally emerges in mid-summer through the fall, and the boletus/porcini (**baravykas**), which tends to emerge in the later summer through the fall.

There are many established paths through the forests and marshes of Lithuania, some of which have educational information posted along them. In a totally strange translation that seems to have caught on throughout the country, these paths are often referred to in English on signs as "cognitive" paths. I imagine this is supposed to convey the idea of being not only educational, but also a place to ponder the meaning of life or perhaps try to figure out hedgehog jokes (see the Humor section).

Lake activities are also very common in Lithuania. Canoeing, kayaking, and even row boating are favored means of boating, since most lakes do not allow motorized vessels. Of course, swimming is an incredibly enjoyable way to refresh yourself on a hot day in Lithuania. Fortunately, lake access throughout the country is quite unrestricted. With few exceptions, if you see a lake, you can go ahead and jump in it. Unlike in litigious countries like the U.S., you will find very few lifeguards and won't be restricted to tiny, roped-off, waist-deep "swimming" areas (I'm looking at you, New York State Office of Parks, Recreation & Historic Preservation…).

Trakai Castle and Lake Galvė

While out in Lithuania's natural areas, you may encounter some of the country's wildlife. Although Lithuania doesn't have incredibly exotic creatures, many of them are either not commonly found in North America or are interesting variations of species with which we are familiar. Some of the notable animals (allegedly) found in Lithuania but not in North America include the cuckoo bird (**gegutė**) and the hedgehog (**ežys**). I write "allegedly" because I'm beginning to suspect that both creatures are part of a country-wide hoax being perpetrated on foreigners akin to an elaborate snipe hunt. I have seen hedgehogs on video, and have heard countless hedgehog jokes, but have never seen one for myself even though I'm told they are fairly common. I have recently been informed that a way to see hedgehogs in Lithuania is to put a bowl of warm milk outside at night and wait for them to come, but this just sounds like another attempt at tricking a gullible foreigner. I have actually heard cuckoos in the forest, but have never seen them. Should you be out in the forest and hear a cuckoo bird, it is Lithuanian superstition to jingle the change in your pocket to receive good fortune.

Cute little hedgehog (ežiukas)

I've been intrigued to see that Lithuanian bumblebees are similar to those in North America, but are black and white instead of black and yellow. (They must not be Steelers fans.) Also be on the lookout for the incredibly cute red squirrels with tufted ears.

Crows (**varnos**) in Lithuania differ a bit from North American crows and amuse me greatly. The most common crows in Lithuania are a smaller variety with a shiny grey head (**kuosa** – jackdaw in English) and a larger variety with a large swath of grey on the body that gives the bird the appearance of wearing a morning jacket (**pilkoji varna** – hooded crow in English). The magpie (šarka), a black and white member of the crow family with a very long tail, might also be spotted. The crows have a caw that is, if not louder, certainly quite different from and perhaps more aggressive sounding than their North American counterparts. Crows in Lithuania appear to inhabit the same echelon of the food chain as seagulls in many other parts of the world, namely the "snatching pastries out of the hands of unsuspecting tourists when their attention is diverted" level.

The stork (**gandras**) is another animal found in Lithuania but not in North America (other than a quite different species of stork found in Florida). These white and black, long-legged birds are commonly seen hunting for frogs and other creatures in marshy areas. Storks are the national bird of Lithuania, enjoy a special status, and play an important role in the country's folklore. They are thought to bring good luck to a family if they nest at their house, and the first stork that you see in a year is said to foretell the type of year you will have (e.g., active, resting… perhaps eating frog legs… mating…).

Storks hunting

I really encourage you to get outside and explore the natural wonder of Lithuania. There are many paths available for you to bike or walk through the forests and by the rivers, lakes, and even the Baltic Sea. If you are very lucky, you just might catch a glimpse of the elusive ežys!

Language

The Lithuanian language is classified as part of the Baltic group of languages (not Slavic like Russian), the only other existing language of which is Latvian. Lithuanian retains many aspects of the early proto-Indo-European language, sharing many of these characteristics with Sanskrit. Lithuanians take pride in their connection to Sanskrit, and also seem to take a somewhat sadistic pride in being one of the most difficult languages to learn. Lucky me! At least it's not in Cyrillic.

History and Significance of the Language

The Lithuanian language is intrinsically connected with the Lithuanian ethnic identity. Throughout Lithuania's history, the use of the language and attempts to suppress its usage have shaped the development of the Lithuanian nation. For most of its early history, the language was not even used by the rulers of Lithuania, as forms of Old Ruthenian and Latin were used. Later, Polish emerged as the language of the ruling class, and Lithuanian remained a language only of the peasants.

The first publication in Lithuanian was a bible translated from German by Martynas Mažvydas in 1547, which also included instructions on how to read Lithuanian. This occurred in the context of the Protestant Reformation, when the use of the local vernacular (in this case Lithuanian) was stressed. Shortly thereafter, the Catholic Church's Counter-Reformation led to the use of Lithuanian in some Catholic church services, thereby incrementally boosting the importance of the language. Still, Lithuanian remained the language of the peasants, and the gentry primarily used Polish. The Polish language continued to be the language of official business and the ruling class of Lithuania until the Russian Empire claimed the country in 1795.

The use of Lithuanian was under attack throughout the period of Russian rule, including periods of being officially banned, and there were many underground efforts to keep the language alive. Publishers in Prussia, and the **knygnešiai** (book smugglers) who transported their publications, played a critical role in maintaining the existence of the language. As momentum for cultural and political freedoms mounted in the late 19th century, the use of the Lithuanian language was a prominent aspect of the movement, gaining a crucial victory in 1904 when the ban on Lithuanian language publications was lifted.

The independent republic that was formed in 1918 was the first to use the Lithuanian language for official purposes. Unfortunately, the return of Russian/Soviet occupation in 1944 led again to suppression of the language, though not to the extent that occurred during the Russian Empire's rule. Again, the language was able to survive and is now flourishing in today's independent country.

The language spoken throughout Lithuania today is based on the Western Aukštaitijan dialect from the Suvalkija region. In the late 19th century, concurrently with the national cultural awakening, a movement to standardize the language emerged, resulting in the form of the language used today. Throughout the ethnographic regions, the older generations often still speak dialects that differ from the modern standard form. The Žemaitijan dialect in particular differs from standard Lithuanian, and is very difficult for other Lithuanians to understand.

Presently, approximately four million Lithuanians and people of Lithuanian origin worldwide speak Lithuanian. Because of its difficulty and relative obscurity, I would hazard a guess that about two people not of Lithuanian origin speak it fluently.

Characteristics of the Language

As I have become more familiar with Lithuanian, I have found certain aspects rather simple and other aspects incredibly complicated. As for simplicity, quite a few words are similar to their counterparts in English and Romance languages, and the structure of sentences is quite flexible, cutting out some difficulties.

One aspect of Lithuanian that benefits non-native speakers tremendously is the widespread use of loanwords from English, especially for modern things. It can actually be pretty comical how easy it is to understand some things in Lithuanian due to this borrowing of words from other languages. You can easily decipher some words by taking off the -as, -is, or -us endings. Thus, "parkas," "restoranas," and "kompiuteris" should make sense to an English speaker. This has led to my use of "Lithuanglish" – just add an "as" or "is" to an English word and surprisingly often it actually is the Lithuanian word for it. In addition, someone familiar with Romance languages should be able to understand quite a few words, such as "bilietas" (ticket), "dušas" (shower), and "servetėlė" (napkin).

Despite these aspects, though, the language strikes me as needlessly complex. One of the reasons the language is so difficult is because the object nouns of a sentence are declinated (the ending is changed) in accordance with how they are being referenced. Put plainly, a word you may know, such as "restoranas", can have fourteen different endings (including plurals) depending on whether you are saying "the restaurant," "to the restaurant," "in the restaurant," "from the restaurant," etc. (restoranas, į restoraną, restorane, iš restorano, etc.). For a speaker of most other languages, this approach is very difficult. How can a noun change like that?!

Dr. Ludwig Zamenhof, the inventor of Esperanto (a constructed language that is quite simple and was intended to be a universal language) lived for a time in the southern Lithuanian town of Veisiejai, and he was familiar with Lithuanian. One can assume he used Lithuanian as a model of how NOT to design a language.

It may be useful to know that the plural versions of nouns will generally end in "-ai" for masculine nouns and "-ės" or "-os" for feminine nouns. Also, like many other languages, Lithuanian has diminutive endings that are added to words to convey cuteness, smallness or tenderness. Masculine words in the diminutive form end in "-ukas" or "utis" and diminutive feminine words end in "-ytė" or "-ėlė".

Since the language is so difficult, and so few foreigners learn the language, Lithuanians are generally very appreciative of even the smallest effort to use their language – a pleasant contrast to a certain cheese-loving people of Western Europe.

Another phenomenon you may notice is that whenever you get two or more Lithuanians in a room (or on the phone), the decibel level seems to increase exponentially. Lithuanians quite often speak in a loud and seemingly aggressive tone that sounds a lot like arguing, even when that is not at all the case. Many times I've thought my wife was arguing with someone, only to find out that they were having a pleasant conversation about how good dinner was or some other random conversation.

To assist you in your attempts to learn some Lithuanian, following is an introduction to pronunciation and some useful phrases.

Pronunciation

Many letters are pronounced as they are in English, and letters have the added bonus of NOT having multiple pronunciations as many letters do in English. There are 9 extra letters in the Lithuanian alphabet (ą, č, ę, ė, į, š, ų, ū, and ž), no "q", "w" or "x", and a whopping 12 vowels. Here are the most important pronunciations to know:

"c" is pronounced "ts", so "pica" is pronounced pi-tsa (sound familiar?)

"č" is pronounced "ch" as in "change"

"ę" is pronounced "a" as in "rat"

"ė" is pronounced "eah" as in "yeah"

"g" is pronounced "g" as in "go"

"į" and "y" are pronounced "ee" as in "tree"

"j" is pronounced "y" as in "yes"

"š" is pronounced "sh" as in "shout"

"ų" and "ū" are both pronounced "oo", as in "boot" (the difference being that "ū" is almost always in the middle of a word, while "ų" is usually at the end)

"ž" is pronounced "zh" like the "s" in "version"

One thing you might notice is that Lithuanian does not have a soft "th" sound. It's a strange twist of fate that the English language version of the country's name has that sound. Many Lithuanians actually end up pronouncing it "Lifuania."

Useful Words and Phrases

English	Lithuanian	Pronunciation (Stress underlined)
Hi	**Labas**	<u>Lah</u>-buss
Good morning	**Labas rytas**	<u>Lah</u>-buss <u>ree</u>-tus
Good day/Hello	**Laba diena**	<u>Lah</u>-bah <u>dyah</u>-na
Good evening	**Labas vakaras**	<u>Lah</u>-buss <u>vah</u>-kah-russ
Goodbye	**Viso gero**	<u>Vi</u>-so <u>geh</u>-ro
Bye*	**Iki**	I-<u>keh</u>
Yes	**Taip**	Typ or tayp
No	**Ne**	Neh
Thanks	**Ačiū**	<u>Ah</u>-choo
You're welcome/ Please	**Prašom**	<u>Prah</u>-shom
Cheers/ Bless you**	**Į sveikatą**	Ee svey-<u>kah</u>-ta
"Bon Appetit"	**Skanaus**	Ska-<u>nous</u>
Tasty	**Skanu**	Ska-<u>nuh</u>
I don't understand	**Nesuprantu**	Neh-suh-prahn-<u>tuh</u>
Lithuanian (lang.)	**Lietuviškai**	Lyeh-<u>tuh</u>-vish-kay
English (lang.)	**Angliškai**	<u>Ahng</u>-glish-kay
I'm American (male)	**Aš Amerikietis**	Ahsh Ah-meyr-i-<u>kyet</u>-iss
I'm American (female)	**Aš Amerikietė**	Ahsh Ah-meyr-i-<u>kyet</u>-eh
I'm Canadian (male)	**Aš Kanadietis**	Ahsh Kah-nah-<u>dyet</u>-iss
I'm Canadian (female)	**Aš Kanadietė**	Ahsh Kah-nah-<u>dyet</u>-eh
Where?	**Kur?**	Kuhr?
Bathroom	**Tualetas**	Twa-let-uss

* Short for "Iki pasimatymo"–"till next time"
** Means "To your Health", said while cheering and after a sneeze

And now one of my favorite Lithuanian phrases: an all-purpose way of expressing surprise, frustration or bewilderment: "**Kas čia dabar?!**" (kas cha dah-bar) – literally "what's here now?!".

Learning the Language

I am currently studying Lithuanian via Skype with Lingua Lituanica (www.lingualit.lt), located in Vilnius. If you are interested in delving into learning Lithuanian, I highly recommend working with this company. In addition to private and group lessons, Lingua Lituanica runs short, intensive courses a couple of times each year that incorporate language and cultural education.

I've found this method of study to be a much more practical approach than working on my own. I've tried many of the instruction books available, and I think it's just too complicated to learn without a skilled instructor. I do however, strongly recommend *Practical Grammar of Lithuanian*, by Meilutė Ramonienė and Joana Pribušauskaitė, as a reference book for learning Lithuanian. As with other books printed in Lithuania, it is available at a very reasonable price in Lithuanian bookstores, but unfortunately it is rather expensive when ordered online in the U.S.

If you have a more casual interest in the language, there is a great podcast series called Lithuanian Out Loud available on iTunes and at http://lithuanian.libsyn.com/. These podcasts teach the language (start from the earliest episodes for the basics) as well as discuss Lithuanian culture, history, art, etc.

Lithuanian Names

Names in Lithuania have many interesting aspects. Essentially all male first names end in -as, -is, or -us, while essentially all female first names end in a vowel. Many names are Lithuanized versions of popular Christian names used throughout the world, but there are also quite a few first names that are unique to Lithuanians. Unique male names, which are mostly the names of historic leaders, include Mindaugas (early leader/King), Gediminas (Grand Duke), Algirdas (Grand Duke, son of Gediminas, father of Jogaila), Kęstutis (Duke, son of Gediminas, father of Vytautas), Vytautas (Grand Duke), Kastytis (fictional character in the legend of Jūratė and Kastytis), Daumantas (the name of two early Dukes), and Tautvydas. Unique female names, which are mostly legendary characters or natural phenomena, include Eglė (legendary Queen of Serpents, also a spruce tree), Jūratė (derived from the word for "sea" and also the name of a legendary mermaid who lived in an amber castle in the Baltic sea), Birutė (real-life wife of Kęstutis, mother of Vytautas, also the pagan equivalent of a saint), Aušra ("dawn") and Aušrinė ("morning star") (Aušra and Aušrinė are both variations of the goddess of the morning), Rasa ("dew"), Aistė (derived from the Baltic tribe Aisčiai), Ieva ("bird cherry tree flower"), Rūta (flowering plant "rue" – symbolizes virginity and is important in folklore), Gabija (goddess of fire), and Austėja (goddess of bees).

Another feature unique to Lithuanian names is that last names (traditionally) have three different forms based on whether someone is a male, an unmarried female, or a married female. Male last names generally end in -as, -is, or -us, unmarried female last names end in -aitė, -ytė, and -ūtė, and married female last names end in -ienė. This is accomplished by adding different suffixes to a root last name, such as Petrausk-, so that the father and son would be Petrauskas, the mother would be Petrauskienė, and the daughter would be Petrauskaitė. Traditionally, a woman would adopt the root from her husband's last name. It is, however, becoming somewhat common for females to not conform to these conventions. Options for women are to adopt a neutral form of female last name that ends in -ė (e.g., Petrauskė), adopt a hyphenated last name (maiden name-husband's last name), or, less frequently, to retain their original name in the traditionally unmarried form.

An amusing aspect of names in Lithuania is that foreign names will be modified so that they use Lithuanian letters, conform to Lithuanian pronunciation, and can be properly declinated. Thus Brad Pitt becomes Bradas Pitas and George Bush becomes Džordžas Bušas. I have myself had some fun encounters with this naming system, as my name requires significant alteration to be a proper male name or else people will declinate my name like I'm a female. One alternative is to change my first name to Kolumbas, which is a name in the proper masculine form (my wife's mother calls me that). Another alternative was strangely presented to me when I signed up for a running race. Someone involved with the race took the liberty of changing the name with which I registered, Columbia Warren, to Kolumbija Varenas.

Food and Drink

One of the best ways to connect with Lithuania and Lithuanians is to enjoy food and drink together. Eating with Lithuanians is a somewhat formal process, so you would do well to know a bit about the customs and etiquette related to dining in Lithuania. Before beginning to eat, it is customary and polite to say "**skanaus**" or "**gero apetito**" (essentially the same as "bon appetit"). If you would like to compliment the food, you should say "**skanu**" ("tasty") or "**labai skanu**" ("very tasty"). I have come to learn that if you are complimenting someone's cooking, you really should say **"labai skanu"** or your sincerity is a bit in doubt. If eating in someone's home, you will likely be offered more food multiple times, because it is considered good manners for hosts to keep offering. It is certainly permissible to politely decline additional food if you have had enough, though you should definitely finish what is on your plate. I've learned the hard way that it okay to decline more food, after repeatedly stuffing myself because I thought it would be rude to say no.

The standard toast in Lithuanian is **"į sveikatą"** ("to your health"). When toasting, you should always make eye contact with the person with whom you are toasting (if there's a specific person). Also, if you would like to eat like a Lithuanian (or continental European in general), you can follow their example and try using the fork in your left hand (turned "upside down") and the knife in your right hand.

Traditional Lithuanian cuisine is based in significant part on the internationally-common meat and potatoes. Mushrooms are also commonly included in dishes, especially in sauces and in southern Lithuania. Lithuanian foods are generally hearty and rather heavy, and best enjoyed during cold days (which are by no means limited to winter – they will routinely occur during the summer as well). Although times are changing, many still treat the midday meal as the main meal of the day.

My initial experience with Lithuanian food was on my first trip to Lithuania, when I met my then-girlfriend's parents for the first time. It was only October, but I got the distinct impression that they were trying to fatten me up for the approaching winter (which I would not actually be experiencing as my visit would only last a few days). Most memorably, my girlfriend's father was treating me to smoked pork products that were literally about half fat. It was certainly a bit of a shock to my American sensibilities, but I was able to consume enough to not come off as a pansy. As I warmed to the cuisine that evening, with the welcome assistance of some homemade vodka (**samanė**), I was introduced to a bounty of delicious dishes prepared by my girlfriend's mother. Today I've certainly overcome any doubts that I may have had, and I always look forward to visiting my wife's family and experiencing real, homemade Lithuanian meals.

Many Lithuanians consider soup (**sriuba**) an essential part of the diet, and it is eaten with nearly every lunch, usually accompanied by potatoes (**bulvės**) or bread (**duona**). (Lithuanians actually differentiate between dark bread (usually rye), which they refer to as duona, and white bread, which they refer to as **batonas**.) A wide variety of hot soups are available, including **burokėlių sriuba** (*borscht*), as well its cold cousin, **šaltibarščiai**, a dish well-suited for warm days made primarily from kefir and beets, along with pieces of hardboiled egg. The white of the kefir and red of the beets leads to a soup that is a potentially off-putting Pepto Bismol pink. Being color-blind in this case will reward you with a creamy, refreshing soup that you should not miss. This dish was probably the biggest hit among the foreign wedding guests of ours who came to Lithuania. As with most soups served in Lithuania, šaltibarščiai is served with steamed potatoes on the side. You are progressing well in your culinary adventures when you are able to eat your potatoes with a fork in one hand and your soup with a spoon in the other hand.

Another dish well-suited for warmer weather that I had until recently not thought much about is **balta mišrainė** – a sort of potato salad-like dish. Mišrainė consists of a mayonnaise base with small pieces of chopped potatoes, carrots, pickles, and peas. More adventurous varieties include herring or mushrooms. Mišrainė really hit the spot during the heat wave that I experienced on my last visit to Lithuania.

Pickled herring (**silkė**) is often included in meals, usually as one of the first courses eaten. Lithuanians have developed a wide variety of preparations for herring, the most common of which is with vinegar, oil and onions. Smoked fish (**rūkyta žuvis**) is sometimes available and is especially common near the coast. It is quite oily and pretty tasty. Smoked eel (**rūkytas ungurys**) is the most prized type of smoked fish.

The most famous Lithuanian dish is **cepelinai** (also known as **didžkukuliai**), a zeppelin-shaped boiled potato dish filled with meat or Lithuanian cheese. I definitely recommend the meat-filled over the cheese-filled. Cepelinai are often served with sour cream (**grietinė**) and fried pieces of bacon (**spirgučiai**). I have grown to love cepelinai, and prefer mine with mushroom sauce, which is quite often available as well. A standard serving in a restaurant consists of two cepelinai, but fortunately for the novice, a **pusė porcijos** (half portion – a single cepelinas) can almost always be ordered. No trip to Lithuania would be complete without trying cepelinai.

My favorite Lithuanian dish is **balandėliai**, the Lithuanian version of the stuffed cabbage dish common throughout Eastern Europe – a ball of meat and rice wrapped in cabbage. This dish is pleasantly moist, as it is prepared by steaming. I especially like balandėliai when they are served with a creamy orange colored carrot-tomato sauce. You will have to get your potato fix with those provided on the side, as this is one of the few traditional dishes that is not made from potatoes.

Another delicious dish is **kugelis**, a baked potato pie akin to a mashed-potato casserole but made from dough of raw potatoes. Kugelis usually has pieces of bacon incorporated in it, and a modern twist on the dish includes chicken wings baked in. This also comes with a bacon and sour cream sauce like most everything else.

Another staple food is **bulviniai blynai**, or potato pancakes, which come in multiple forms and with savory toppings. Similarly, crêpes, referred to in Lithuania as **blyneliai** or **lietiniai** (and sometimes just "pancakes"), are a popular dish in both sweet and savory forms. You may have to search pretty hard if you have a craving for American-style pancakes.

One dish that has not enchanted me after a couple of attempts is **vėdarai**, a mashed potato concoction (similar to kugelis) filling a casing made of pig large intestines. Mmmmm… piggy! If this style of vėdarai doesn't do the trick for you, there is apparently another (original) version from the Aukštaitija region that is pig intestines filled with fresh pig's blood. Double piggy!

Kibinai, a fairly greasy meat-filled pastry, is another tasty traditional dish that is common, but it is not of Lithuanian origin. Instead, this dish originated with the Karaims (Karaites), an ethnic group from the Crimea who were brought to Lithuania in the 14th century by Vytautas the Great.

International cuisine has made significant inroads in Lithuania, the most prominent addition being pizza (**pica**). The quality of pizza offered is actually quite good, with the most common style being a rather thin, crisp crust. Lithuanians tend to adulterate their pizzas by squeezing copious amounts of pink or white mayonnaise-based sauces all over them, then eating them with a fork and knife.

Another food from abroad (Armenia) that has actually been in Lithuania for a while is **šašlykai** (shish kebab). It is much less common in restaurants, but a favorite for grilling – Lithuanians think of šašlykas as a quintessential dish to prepare while being out in nature. There is also the ever-present fast food **kebabai** (essentially gyros), which is often served out of roadside stands or small shops in the cities.

Lithuania has a few notable dessert items. The most famous and unique, generally reserved for special occasions, is **šakotis** – sweet eggy dough hardened into a shape reminiscent of a Christmas tree. Šakotis is prepared by dribbling the dough onto a slowly rotating rod, with the dough running down and hardening into what look like branches. Šakočiai vary in size from small (maybe six inches) to enormous (I've seen ones as tall as a person).

Šakotis in the process of being made

Other more common desserts include **spurgos**, round fried doughnuts often with **varškė** (a creamy cottage cheese) inside. I give spurgos a big thumbs up, but of course I'm a sucker for doughnuts. There are also plenty of delicious cakes and tarts to try – I especially like the Lithuanian version of cheesecake made with varškė. Lithuanian desserts are often a bit less sweet than desserts in North America.

Lithuania has a good domestic beer (**alus**) scene, which seems to be becoming more crowded on each visit, especially with the emergence of a prominent microbrew contingent. In addition, many international brands that are likely unfamiliar to an American are pouring into the Lithuanian market. Grimbergen, from Belgium, was the latest beer from abroad being heavily promoted on my last trip. Domestically-produced beer is a tremendous value, often being about the same price in a restaurant as water or juice. Major domestic (although all foreign-owned) beer brands include Švyturys in Klaipėda, Utenos in Utena, and Kalnapilis in Panevėžys. My stand-by favorite alus is **Švyturys Ekstra**, a smooth, light, full-flavored lager with fairly heavy carbonation and a nice head. Unlike in North America, "light" beers in Lithuania refer to the color, not the strength or calorie content.[7] In fact, even the light (pale) beers in Lithuania are surprisingly strong, often exceeding 5% alcohol by volume. Beer aficionados will likely want to explore the products of the many smaller brewers of the country, some of which are available in restaurants.

Lithuania provides many tempting "beer snacks" (**užkandžiai prie alaus**) to accompany an afternoon or evening sipping alus with friends. My top choice is always **kepta duona** – delicious strips of crisp, fried dark bread generally rubbed with garlic (**česnakas**). Kepta duona also commonly comes covered with a white sauce and cheese (**sūris**), but I prefer to opt for the ver-

---

[7] My brother-in-law likes to remind me of how American beer and having sex on a beach are similar: both are f**king close to water…

sion without cheese (I'm already eating <u>fried</u> bread!). Many other beer snack options abound, including thin strips of **rūkytos ausys** (smoked pig ears), **rauginatas agurkas** (pickles) and split pea porridge with bacon (of course). I'm not such a fan of the pig ears – it's just crunchy cartilage with a light smoky flavor.

The adventurous imbiber will have plenty of strong drinks to explore, including of course the ever-present **degtinė** (vodka). The Lithuanian brand **Stumbras** produces a variety of vodkas, including a version of the traditional moonshine (**samanė**), which is essentially vodka with a bit of a bready flavor. Stumbras also produces a plethora of **trauktinės** (bitter liqueurs), including my favorite, **Žalios Devynerios** (Green Nines), an herbal liqueur reminiscent of some of the classics produced in European monasteries (there is also the original "Three Nines" and "Red Nines"). Other Lithuanian trauktinės include **starka**, which is sort of like whiskey (**viskis**)[8], and **Malūnininkų**, a very strong bitter that will challenge your taste buds with bold flavors. Lithuania also produces fine honey liqueur, **midus** (mead), with many different varieties that range from mild to strong, in terms of both taste and alcohol content. Another traditional honey liqueur, **krupnikas**, differs from midus in that it is quite sweet, contains spices, and is usually much higher in alcohol content. For some reason, brandy (**brendis**) is also very popular in Lithuania, and is a very common drink at festive occasions.

While on this subject: you may notice an odd habit of Lithuanians in connection with drinking. Lithuanians sometimes flick

---

[8] Viskis – not to be confused with **viskas**, which means "everything". Clerks at stores and waiters sometimes ask: "Viskas?" ("Is that everything?"). They are not offering you whiskey to go along with the candy bar and tank of gas as I first thought.

their forefinger or middle finger to their neck (where the jaw meets the neck) when referring to drinking. The story I've been told is that during the time of the Russian Empire, a person who was designated as a hero by the Tsar would have a symbol tattooed on his neck that indicated such status. With the tattoo (which would be referenced with the finger flick) he could drink for free in any tavern in the empire. This story may be apocryphal, but it's one of those customs you can use to fit in with the locals.

An interesting non-alcoholic (technically very low alcohol) drink found in Lithuania is **gira** (also known as kvass in other parts of Europe). This cold beverage is made (in its original form – many brands today use shortcuts) by fermenting dark bread and sugar together into a malty carbonated drink. During the warmer months, gira is often sold out of kitschy olde tyme carts. I also recommend trying **gilių kava**, or "acorn coffee," which is ground acorn and sweetened milk. It has an interesting flavor and is quite tasty. Another interesting flavor to seek out is that of sea buckthorn berry juice (**šaltalankis**). I recommend trying a drink or sauce made from this berry, which has extremely high levels of vitamin C (15 times that of oranges) and many other healthy attributes. Various fruit juices, or compotes (**kompotas**), are also quite popular. Juices and water are generally served at room temperature and without ice, not cold. On one of my first visits to Lithuania, my wife's mother actually profusely apologized because the juice was cold, having been kept in the refrigerator. I was a bit confused by that! There are also plenty of mineral waters available in stores, but if you prefer a water with very low minerality (as I do), I recommend Neptūnas brand.

For your caffeine fix, coffee (**kava**) is available in most cafés and restaurants, as well as some actual coffee shops. Most coffee in Lithuania, and throughout Europe, comes in smaller sizes than Americans are used to and is often not available to go, though this option is becoming more common. Coffee Inn coffee shops, of which there are a few in the old town of Vilnius, do serve large sized coffees that can be taken to go. If you are served coffee in someone's home, you will likely have either French press style or what I know as "cowboy coffee" – that is, ground coffee that has been mixed directly with hot water in the cup – instead of the drip coffee that is standard in American homes. Although it may seem odd, the coffee is actually so finely ground that it ends up settling into a nearly solid sludge at the bottom of the cup and doesn't cause a problem. Tea (**arbata**) is also very popular in Lithuania, and many great varieties of herbal teas are available. If you're looking for an "energy drink," I recommend Battery brand energy drinks.

Sports and Recreation

Sport in Lithuania is all about basketball, with everything else vying for any leftover interest among sports fans.

Basketball

Virtually any conversation with a Lithuanian will eventually lead to the subject of basketball, which, as you will undoubtedly be informed during that conversation, is the "second religion" of Lithuania. (The first religion, if I'm not mistaken, is frowning.) Indeed, basketball is very popular in Lithuania and the country has experienced some significant successes on the world stage since the restoration of independence: three bronze medals (and two fourth place finishes) in the Olympics; a bronze in the

FIBA World Championships; and a championship and bronze in EuroBasket. Lithuanians also made up substantial portions of successful Soviet teams of the past. The most notable internationally recognized Lithuanian basketball players are Žydrūnas Ilgauskas and Arvydas Sabonis, the latter of whom was recently inducted into the Naismith Basketball Hall of Fame.

Crowd celebrating a basketball victory in the Kaunas Town Hall Square

Lithuania has a national basketball league, the LKL, and some of the teams in that league also compete internationally in the Baltic Basketball League, the VTB United League (Eastern and Northern Europe), and the Euroleague. By far the most successful and well-known teams in Lithuania are Žalgiris of Kaunas and Lietuvos Rytas of Vilnius.

Formed in 1944, Žalgiris has a storied past. With Arvydas Sabonis as its star, Žalgiris was a dominant team in the Soviet league and in Europe during the mid-1980s, and came to be seen as the *de facto* Lithuanian national team. During the

47

independence movement and throughout the 1990s, Žalgiris was an important source of national pride.

Žalgiris won every LKL championship during the 1990s, but in the 21st century, it has had to battle Lietuvos Rytas for the top spot. Since the 2000 season, every final has been between these two teams, with a fairly even split of championships between them. There is a definite rivalry between Vilnius and Kaunas, similar to the rivalry between New York and Boston. Like New York-Boston, sports is but one aspect of the rivalry felt between the two, with Kaunas playing the role of the smaller, somewhat underdog like Boston. Lietuvos Rytas has recently been the better financed team, but Žalgiris retains more of a fanbase throughout the country.

Lietuvos Rytas plays in the Siemens Arena, located just outside Vilnius near the Ozas shopping mall. Žalgiris plays in the brand new Žalgiris Arena located on an island in the Nemunas river across from the Akropolis shopping mall in Kaunas.

Other Sports

Lithuania seems to specialize in what might be termed "burly man" sports. There are always a few Lithuanians vying for the top in strongman competitions. Žydrūnas Savickas, the 2009 and 2010 World's Strongest Man (2nd in 2011), is considered one of the sport's best athletes ever. Also, three of Lithuania's four Olympic gold medals since restoration of independence have come in discus. One can assume that cepelinai figure prominently in the training diets of such girth-endowed athletes.

As in the rest of Europe, soccer (football) and Formula 1 racing are fairly popular, certainly more so than in the U.S. Surprisingly, for how much Lithuanians love lakes and swimming, I am not aware of competitive swimming being very important in Lithuania. Tennis is somewhat popular, and there is a promising young player named Ričardas Berankis playing on the ATP World Tour.

Strangely, beach volleyball seems to be gaining some significant popularity. Beach volleyball courts seem to be springing up all over the place (quite often not on actual beaches).

Lithuania is also quite strong in competitive dancing, and dancing is very popular among the general population. The country has produced successful ballroom dancing and ice dancing teams that compete internationally.

Lithuanians also seem to really like to fish, which makes sense in that it combines several things that Lithuanians enjoy: being in nature, drinking beer, lakes, sitting quietly (presumably while frowning), and spending time away from their wives.

Interestingly, each of the Baltic countries seems to have their one sport that is a national obsession. Lithuania has basketball, while Latvians love hockey and Estonians love cross-country skiing.

Humor

Some Lithuanian humor tends to be rather dark and absurd. One of the most famous (common) kinds of jokes in Lithuania, which are almost completely inexplicable to outsiders, are jokes about a "little hedgehog" (**ežiukas**). These are usually one sentence jokes centered around the hedgehog minding his own business, only to have some absurd, sometimes unfortunate, incident occur. Examples include:

- Once a little hedgehog was walking through the forest and fell into a hole – and there were Germans!
- Once a little hedgehog was walking through the forest, then he forgot how to breathe and died.
- Once a little hedgehog was walking through the desert carrying two buckets of sand.
- Once a little hedgehog was walking through the forest, then he saw a burning tank, got inside it and burned alive.

Obviously, the humor of these is quite difficult to understand, but it is clear that there are some dark pessimistic elements going on and also some culture specific references. Also note that the joke can open up many questions about how this scenario came to be – consider for instance the Germans in a hole in the woods!

One reasonable attempt at explaining these jokes is based on the idea that the hedgehog is a somewhat overlooked forest creature that does not have traits attributed to it like other animals (e.g., sly fox, wise owl, cruel wolf, etc.). Instead, the hedgehog seems to be a sort of innocent, naive character who gets in nobody's way. It seems a rather unfair twist of fate that the hedgehog ends up in what are often life-threatening predicaments. While I haven't heard anyone explicitly make a connection, I have to imagine there is some commentary on the Lithuanian character wrapped up in these jokes.

Lithuanians also like to tell Estonian jokes, in the same way that Americans tell Polish or blonde jokes and Canadians tell Newfie jokes. The stereotype about Estonians is that they are phlegmatic, or a bit slow in their decision-making process. A great example: On Estonian roads, next to the road sign indicating "Entering Traffic Circle" is another sign that states "No more than three times around permitted." Also: Estonians don't buy alcohol, they just buy juice and it turns to alcohol before they get around to finishing it.

Customs

It is worth keeping in mind that, as a foreigner, you will likely be scrutinized a bit for how you comport yourself. If you are American, as you travel in Lithuania do keep in mind that a negative stereotype of Americans worldwide is that we are loud, arrogant, lazy, boorish, stupid, spoiled, McDonald's-burger-munching, cheap-beer-swilling fatsos. Though they are incredibly welcoming and kind, Lithuanians aren't immune to holding this view of Americans to a certain extent. Anything you can do to counteract that stereotype while abroad is certainly helpful.

There are a few customs that will be very helpful for you to know in order to get along well in Lithuania without causing offense. Many of these are based on superstitions and the avoidance of bad luck. There are also customs that are useful to know just because you might see something and wonder what is going on. Customs related to dining have been discussed already in the Food and Drink section.

- It is important to keep eye contact with the person to whom or with whom you are toasting with a drink. It is considered to cause bad luck if you do not have eye contact when toasting.

- You should not shake hands across a threshold (through a doorway), since this is considered to cause bad luck.

- It is very customary in Lithuania to bring small gifts, usually chocolate, other sweets, or alcohol, when visiting someone. Some Lithuanians bring flowers when visiting (especially when visiting a female host), while others reserve flowers for special occasions such as birthdays and name days. If flowers are given to a host or for a celebratory occasion (birthday, name day, wedding, anniversary, etc.), it is necessary to give an odd number of flowers, as an even number of flowers is associated with death and funerals.

- It is considered impolite to point, especially with the index finger as is customary in North America. Referencing something should be done with an open handed gesture or with a nod.

- You will likely see padlocks all over the railings of bridges. These have been placed there in connection with weddings as a symbol of the permanent bond of marriage. Married couples attach the lock and then throw the key(s) into the river or stream below. This is actually a very recent custom in Lithuania. Some bridges now have a huge number of locks on them, posing an interesting engineering challenge due to the weight. If you happen to be in Druskininkai, look out for our lock on the small bridge where the Ratnyčia flows into the Nemunas (near the Kolonada restaurant)!

- Also related to bridges, it is tradition for grooms to carry their brides over bridges after the wedding ceremony. I got off easy with only carrying my wife over the aforementioned bridge, which is quite short.

Holidays

Lithuanians celebrate a variety of holidays that are generally patriotic or religious, and many include some elements of paganism thrown in for good measure. One interesting phenomenon in Lithuania is that, instead of having "observed" holidays on Mondays or Fridays as in the U.S. and Canada, many businesses and the government will have employees work on a Saturday in order to create a three- or four-day weekend out of a holiday that falls on a Tuesday or Thursday.

- December 31/January 1 – New Year's (**Naujieji Metai**) – New Year's Eve and Day is a big celebration for Lithuanians. This is partly a holdover from Soviet times, because Christmas could not be widely celebrated and a lot of the celebration was transferred to New Year's.

- February 16 – Day of Independence (**Nepriklausomybės diena**) – This is the commemoration of the declaration of independence in 1918.

- March 8 – International Women's Day (**Moters diena**) – This holiday, a holdover from Soviet times that is no longer an official state holiday, has transformed from a communist holiday to a general day of honoring women. On this day, men give flowers (often tulips) to women.

- March 11 – Independence Restoration Day (**Nepriklausomybės atkūrimo diena**) – This day commemorates the declaration of the restoration of Lithuania's independence in 1990.

- Easter (**Velykos**) (Date varies) – This is the traditional Easter holiday, and is more prominent for Lithuanians, even non-religious ones, than it is for the general U.S. population.

- May 1 – International Workers' Day (also known as May Day) – This holiday, which celebrates workers and workers' movements, is to a certain extent a Soviet holdover.

- Mother's Day (First Sunday in May) and Father's Day (First Sunday in June)

- June 24 – St. John's Day (**Joninės** – Christian name), Day of Dew (**Rasos** – original pagan name) – This is the day of celebration that coincides with the traditional Midsummer's Eve, and is often celebrated with bonfires and outdoor events.

- July 6 – King Mindaugas crowning/ Statehood day (**Karaliaus Mindaugo karūnavimo/valstybės diena**)– Celebrates the crowning of the one internationally recognized King of Lithuania in 1253.

- August 15 – Assumption Day (**Žolinė**) – This is a Catholic holiday celebrating the assumption of Mary to Heaven, but has a very pagan-sounding name in Lithuanian.

- November 1 – All Saints Day (**Visų šventųjų diena**) – This holiday, although at essentially the same time as, and based on the same concept as, Halloween, is a somber event commemorating one's deceased ancestors, and usually involves visiting and lighting candles on their graves.

- December 25 and 26 – Christmas (**Kalėdos**) – Lithuanian Christmas is less commercial and more family-oriented than in North America. The celebration begins with a dinner on Christmas Eve (**Kūčios**), the night of the 24th, which traditionally consists of 12 small dishes without meat or dairy. One of the unique traditional dishes is **kūčiukai** (small round cracker-like things) that are soaked in bowls of **aguonų pienas** (poppy seed milk). Dinner is followed by a number of fortune-telling games, including drawing straws from under the tablecloth to determine one's longevity. On Christmas day, a small number of gifts are exchanged, which have been kept under the Christmas tree (**eglė** or **eglutė**). Eating and celebrating continue on through the 26th.

Throughout the year, each person also celebrates his or her "Name Day" (**vardadienis**).

Part II

Places to Visit

Vilnius

(Population: approx. 560,000)

View over the Old Town of Vilnius

The city of Vilnius[9] has a founding legend that stretches back to Grand Duke Gediminas in the early 14th century. While on a hunting trip in the area of present-day Vilnius, Gediminas is said to have slept in a holy oak grove and dreamt of an iron wolf howling on the top of what is now Gediminas Hill. Gediminas was told by a pagan priest that this vision was a directive to found a city at that location, and that the city would be famed throughout the world. In 1320, Gediminas transferred his royal court from Trakai to Vilnius.

Vilnius certainly became a prominent city with far-reaching influence. After a long and complicated history that has alternated between glorious and tragic, Vilnius is now the financial and

---

[9] Vilnius is pronounced "Vil-nus", with a very slight "y" sound like "Vilnyus," not "Vil-nee-us".

cultural center of 21st century Lithuania. As a city that has experienced a great deal of war and many years of foreign rule, quite a bit of the physical history is hidden or has been destroyed; however, a surprising number of historical buildings remain, considering the destructive past. The most visible parts of the city's history are found in the old town section (**senamiestis**) of the city, which is a wonderful area to wander about and explore. The city is renowned for its late Baroque architecture, which is on full display throughout the senamiestis.

The city has experienced so much population upheaval that the visible remnants of those populations barely scratch the surface at telling their stories. The city has at various times had significant populations of Lithuanians, Poles, Russians and Jews. I highly recommend the book *Vilnius: City of Strangers* by Laimonas Briedis (available online in the U.S. and for much cheaper in Lithuanian bookstores), which paints a very interesting portrait of the many faces of this city as well as the country as a whole.

Probably the best approach to getting to know Vilnius is to take a leisurely stroll through the Old Town. Exploring the winding streets and peering into alleyways will provide ample opportunity to dig into the history and architecture of the city. It will soon become evident that Vilnius is still a city in transition, with some run-down buildings, even ruins, standing side-by-side with beautifully restored buildings and newly-built modern structures. Many courtyards are also accessible to the public, and can present a very interesting view into the past and present life of Vilnius residents. (Just try to overlook the graffiti that covers a significant number of buildings.) As an example of this, I recently followed chalk-drawn advertisements for an art exhibition in the center of Vilnius, only to find myself in the second floor of an unrenovated shell of a building, with squatters presenting their art. There's a lot to be found in Vilnius if you look for it!

Another thing I really like about Vilnius is that it is a bit off the tourist trail compared to other capital cities. Unlike Riga and Tallinn, it is not as geared to, nor as or overrun by, tourists, so it is easier to get a sense of how the residents actually live. If you are out on a Friday or Saturday night, though, you will almost definitely encounter some soused Brits wandering about having a stag or hen party (bachelor or bachelorette party).

Lest you think Vilnius is all about history and old buildings, one need only look across the Neris River to see otherwise. Vilnius is home to a great deal of commercial and financial activity, and the gleaming new buildings in **Šnipiškės** (the financial district) display the prosperity that has come to the country.

Financial district in Vilnius with the Europa Tower (the tallest building in the Baltic States) second from the left

Plenty of information about Vilnius is available on the city's official tourism website at www.vilnius-tourism.lt. Information about and links to websites for almost all specific attractions listed in this section can be found on this Vilnius site. The Vilnius tourism website is the best source for opening times and admission prices, as some of the attraction websites do not have all this information available in the English language pages. Tourism offices are located at the airport, the train station, in the Old Town Hall, at 22 Vilnaus gatvė, and in a kiosk at Cathedral Square.

A somewhat useful website for museums throughout Vilnius and Lithuania can be found at www.muziejai.lt.

Senamiestis (Old Town)

The Old Town is the heart of tourism in Vilnius and has been placed on the list of UNESCO World Heritage sites. Pilies gatvė/Didžioji gatvė/Aušros Vartų gatvė is the main pedestrian thoroughfare through the Old Town. There are many important and historic buildings along this stretch of streets, especially on Pilies gatvė. Vokiečių gatvė is another important street that intersects with Didžioji gatvė at the Rotušės aikštė (the old town hall square). Stiklių gatvė and Literatų gatvė are a couple of the many interesting side streets I would recommend exploring.

Much of the area surrounding Vokiečių (German) gatvė, including Žydų (Jewish) gatvė, encompasses the old Jewish district. (Although these street names are a bit strange in combination, the German district of Vilnius had previously been located in this area as well, and the Lutheran church is still located on Vokiečių gatvė.) Of note is the large courtyard surrounded by Vokiečių, Žydų, Stiklių, and Dominikonų, and accessible through various short alleyways. This courtyard was the center of Jewish life in Vilnius and the site of the Great Synagogue, built in the 1630s and demolished by the Soviets in the 1950s after it sustained significant damage during WWII.

There is plenty to explore in Vilnius, and I can't describe it all, but in this section I will provide you with some of my recommendations.

Vilnius, one of the greenest capitals in Europe

Churches

Vilnius is a city of churches, with a wide array spread throughout the Old Town and beyond. Many of these churches date from the 17th and 18th centuries, and most of those that date from earlier were significantly renovated and altered within that time frame. As a result, the Baroque style abounds, with pastel exteriors and ornate interiors being common.

Poles (who dominated the city for a couple of centuries) and ethnic Lithuanians are almost exclusively Catholic, so many of the churches in Vilnius are Catholic. There are also a number of Russian Orthodox churches, reflecting the long period of Russian control of Vilnius. There are a few Protestant churches scattered about as well. One lone synagogue remains in Vilnius, located at Pylimo g. 39.

As one would imagine, during the Soviet occupation churches were confiscated and converted into other uses, including recreational halls, art galleries, and warehouses. Since independence, many churches have undergone considerable restoration. Some have been reclaimed for religious uses and others now have secular uses. Most are open to the public without admission, a few have paid admission, and some are closed to the public. Below are the churches that I recommend you make a point of visiting.

You can find the churches described below on the Vilnius Places of Interest map at www.experiencinglithuania.com.

▲ Vilnius Cathedral/Chapel of St. Casimir
(Katedros aikštė 1)
The Vilnius Cathedral (the Cathedral of St. Stanislaus and St. Ladislau) is the largest and one of the most impressive churches in Vilnius. Church structures have been at this location since the 13th century, and the current structure is mostly comprised of elements from the late 18th century. Ironically, since Vilnius is said to have been founded based on guidance from a pagan priest, the Christian structures on the site displaced a pagan temple and holy oak grove that previously stood there.

View of Vilnius Cathedral from the side, showing the Chapel of Saint Casimir on the right

The Cathedral proper is surrounded by five chapels, the most famous of which is the Chapel of St. Casimir. This chapel is dedicated to, and holds the remains of, Saint Casimir, the patron saint of Lithuania. Casimir was a grandson of Jogaila (King of Poland and Grand Duke of Lithuania) and was in line for the Polish throne, but died of tuberculosis in 1484. Soon after his death, Casimir's body became associated with many miracles, and he was eventually canonized in 1602. There are many interesting features of the chapel, but perhaps the most interesting is a painting called The Three-Handed St. Casimir, which is believed by some to work miracles. The painting is so-named because a hand that was painted, then covered over with the hand in a different position, now shows through on the canvas, giving the appearance of Casimir having three hands.

Tours of the vaults below the Cathedral are available in English, although they sometimes require advance booking. The office arranging tours is located in the south entrance of the Cathedral (the side entrance near the Chapel of St. Casimir). The tour is very worth taking if possible, as the vaults contain the remains of a variety of nobles and the archeological aspects are very interesting. A fresco dating from the late 14th century is also visible in the vaults.

▲ Parish Church of Saints John the Baptist and John the Evangelist
(Šv. Jono gatvė 12)
This church is located within the confines of Vilnius University; therefore it is only accessible through the courtyards (see the Vilnius University Courtyards section). It is one of the more impressive churches in Vilnius, both inside and out. The church is also one of the oldest in Vilnius, with some Gothic elements (most notably the windows in the facade) from the early 15th century remaining. Most of the church's present appearance dates to the mid-18th century, when the church was rebuilt after a fire. The freestanding bell tower is visible high above Pilies g., at the corner of Pilies g. and Šv. Jono g. The bell tower is now accessible to visitors, as described below in the Other Panoramic Viewing Spots section.

▲ Church of Saint Anne/ Church of St. Francis of Assisi (Bernardine Church)
(Maironio gatvė 10)
Probably the most famous church in Vilnius besides the Cathedral, miniscule Saint Anne is an impressive example of Lithuanian Gothic architecture. Pieced together from red bricks, many of which were carved into decorative shapes, the facade resembles a mini version of much larger Gothic churches in Western Europe. Napoleon is said to have expressed his desire

to take the church home with him in the palm of his hand. As with other churches, St. Anne exhibits styles from multiple periods: the facade remains from the 16th century from around the time the church was first built, the Baroque interior altars date from the 18th century, and the accompanying bell tower is a Neo-Gothic structure dating from the late 19th century.

Church of Saint Anne (left), Church of St. Francis of Assisi (middle), and 19th century bell tower (right)

Standing behind and to the side of the Church of St. Anne is the Church of St. Francis of Assisi (often referred to as the Bernardine Church). This church also exhibits Gothic architecture from the 16th century (most impressively, a tower in the rear of the church) but leaves a distinctly Baroque impression due to a restyled upper part of the facade. Much of the interior also includes Baroque elements from the 18th century.

Church of St. Casimir

▲ Church of St. Casimir

(Didžioji gatvė 34)

The Church of St. Casimir was the first Baroque church in Lithuania, built in 1604-1632 and significantly renovated after a fire in the 18th century. This large and prominent church near the Rotušės aikštė features an interesting crown-like top with a Lithuanian-style cross. In one of the most offensive uses of a church during Soviet times, this church was turned into a museum of atheism during that period.

▲ Church of St. Nicholas

(Šv. Mikalojaus gatvė 4)

The Church of St. Nicholas is one of the oldest extant churches in Lithuania, first built in the 14th century by Germans while paganism was still dominant in Lithuania. The church exhibits significant Gothic elements with some Baroque elements from reconstructions in the 18th and 19th centuries. During the period between WWI and WWII, when Vilnius was part of Poland, this was the only church with services performed in Lithuanian.

▲ Church of St. Catherine
(Vilniaus gatvė 30)
This beautiful late Baroque church was the first to be renovated after independence. The church no longer serves a religious function, but is instead a venue for concerts and exhibitions.

▲ Orthodox Church of St. Nicholas
(Didžioji gatvė 12)
This elaborate and well-restored Russian Orthodox church is a prominent site on Didžioji gatvė. The original structure dates from the mid-19th century, while the chapel on the left of the facade, and the bell tower on the right of the facade, date from 1865. Unfortunately, these two structures were built in honor of Nikolai Mouraviev, the Russian Governor-General of Vilnius, who played a leading role in crushing the 1863-4 Lithuanian rebellion.

▲ Church of St. Peter and St. Paul
(Antakalnio gatvė 1)
This church is located about a kilometer up the street from the National Museum. The church is often heralded as having one of the most impressive interiors of any church in Vilnius. Begun in 1668, the church was decorated with remarkable stucco sculptures by Italian craftsmen during 1677-86. These sculptures remain, as well as some impressive paintings and an elaborate chandelier in the shape of a sailing vessel. Since it is set outside the old town in the opposite direction from the new town, it is a bit out of the way if you are on foot, and is worth skipping if you are short on time.

Gates of Dawn, with the icon of the Virgin Mary visible through the window

▲ Gates of Dawn (Aušros Vartai)

(Aušros Vartų gatvė 12)

At the end of Aušros Vartų gatvė lies the Gates of Dawn, the only remaining gate from the city's walls that were built in the 16th century. The gate is now most famous for the Chapel of the Gates of Dawn and the icon of the Virgin Mary contained therein. The icon is visible through a large window above the gate, and is believed to have miracle working powers. Due to a tradition of miracles (and because it is a tourist attraction), there are often a few disfigured or crippled beggars under and around the gate.

Museums

You can find the museums described below on the Vilnius Places of Interest map at www.experiencinglithuania.com.

▲ Museum of Genocide Victims (KGB Museum)

This museum, which should be on your list to visit, is located in the former KGB building just off of Gedimino prospektas in the Naujamiestis (new city). The museum is well set up and showcases materials related to the Soviet oppression of Lithuanians during the occupation, and provides a lot of information in English. Displays explore the activities of the Lithuanian partisan resistance known as the Forest Brothers, as well as the mass deportations to Siberia. Local activities of the KGB are also presented, including the actual cells and execution chambers in the basement of the building. A visit to this museum is very helpful in understanding the lives of Lithuanians during the Soviet occupation, especially the first, most brutal period under Stalin.

It is important to note that this museum is almost exclusively related to the treatment of ethnic Lithuanians under the Soviet regime, and does not cover the Holocaust of Lithuania's Jews under the Nazis. Given the magnitude of the genocide of the Jews in Lithuania, the lack of virtually any reference to it is a bit galling, but it is not the subject matter of the museum. Those seeking exhibitions related to the Holocaust will need to go to the Holocaust Museum (in Vilnius and discussed below), the Paneriai Memorial Museum (on the outskirts of Vilnius) or the museum at the Ninth Fort outside of Kaunas.

The museum's website is at www.genocid.lt/muziejus. The museum is closed on Mondays and Tuesdays, and adult admission is 6LTL. The entrance to the museum is slightly hidden, as it is located on the side of the building facing a small park area (technically on Aukų gatvė), not directly on Gedimino prospektas.

▲ National Museum

This museum presents a wide range of artifacts and art related to the history of Lithuania. The museum is situated just a few steps from Cathedral Square, at the base of Pilies kalnas and facing the river, on Arsenalo gatvė. While it is worth a visit of an hour or two, it is certainly a bit sparser than the national museums of many other countries. The funicular up to the upper castle on Pilies kalnas is located at the museum.

The National Museum's website is at www.lnm.lt. The museum is closed on Mondays year round, as well as on Tuesdays from October through April. Admission is 5LTL for adults.

▲ Church Heritage Museum

The Church Heritage Museum, located in the Church of St. Michael at Šv. Mykolo g. 9 very near the Church of St. Anne, contains artifacts from the treasury of the Vilnius Cathedral. The pieces have an amazing history of having been walled off in the Cathedral until after Lithuania regained its independence from the Soviet Union.

The museum is closed on Sundays and Mondays, and admission is 9LTL. The museum's website is available at www.bpmuziejus.lt.

▲ Vilna Gaon Jewish State Museum

The Jewish State Museum runs multiple facilities that serve to commemorate and celebrate Jewish culture in Lithuania.

The Holocaust Exhibition, known as the Green House, staffed by helpful volunteers, is a modest museum set in a small green house that presents materials related to the genocide of Jews in Lithuania. It is located at Pamėkalnio g. 12, hidden off the street up a short driveway. I found it based on directions from the staff at the History Exhibitions of the Jewish State Museum, located down the street at Pylimo g. 4.

The History Exhibitions and Gallery of the Righteous, also a modest museum, is set in a large building with materials about Jewish culture in Lithuania. The exhibition on the top floor, presenting pictures and stories of Lithuanians who aided Jews during the Nazi occupation and given the designation Righteous among the Nations, is particularly inspiring. Unfortunately, the museum's website lists this museum as closed. I do not know if this is a temporary or permanent closure.

The Jewish State Museum also hosts the Tolerance Center, another museum dedicated to Litvak culture, and a small museum at the site of the Paneriai massacre.

The website for all museums is at www.jmuseum.lt. Admission is free to the Paneriai Memorial Museum and 5LTL to each of the Green House and Tolerance Center. All of the museums are closed on Saturdays and the Paneriai Memorial Museum is also closed on Fridays.

Other Sites

You can find the sites described below on the Vilnius Places of Interest map at www.experiencinglithuania.com.

▲ Vilnius University Courtyards

The 13 courtyards of Vilnius University offer an interesting glimpse into this old educational institution, showcasing some examples of exceptional architecture from the 18th and 19th centuries. The university, founded in 1589, is the oldest in the Baltic countries, and one of the oldest in Eastern Europe. There is a charge of 5LTL to enter the courtyards through the public entrance at Universiteto g. 3, and this includes entry to the Parish Church of Saints John the Baptist and John the Evangelist. I have heard, however, that it is possible to wander through the courtyards without paying, but you will not receive a map. I can't attest to whether this is permitted or not, but it's worth looking into.

▲ Presidential Palace

Right across the street from the entrance to the Vilnius University courtyards is the Presidential Palace. It was originally built in the 16th century, with significant reconstruction in the 18th century. The Palace was used by the Russian Governor General during the long rule of the Russian Empire, and was used by the French during Napoleon's invasion.

▲ Rotušė and Rotušės aikštė

Situated at the intersection of Vokiečių g., Didžioji g. and Aušros Vartų g., the Rotušė (town hall) is a focal point for the area. If you look closely, you will find a plaque on the Rotušė with a quote of Džordžas Bušas (George Bush) from his historic visit to Lithuania after the country joined NATO. The square (Rotušės aikštė) is one of the areas in Vilnius where big events take place, and has really nice outdoor seating areas for the surrounding restaurants.

▲ Cathedral Square (Katedros aikštė)

Cathedral Square is an expansive square that includes the Cathedral, a bell tower, the newly-recreated Lower Castle, and some sculptures. This is a large meeting area where many events take place.

The bell tower includes one of the old castle wall towers as its base. Near the bell tower and the Cathedral is a square stone with a picture of a star on it. According to local tradition, standing on the stone and spinning 360 degrees while making a wish will make that wish come true.

The Lower Castle (or Palace of the Grand Dukes of Lithuania) in the square today is a newly-completed reproduction of the palace that stood on that spot from the early 16th century until it was destroyed by the Russians in 1795. There are no known records of the original appearance of the palace, so this reproduction is actually just an approximation. The palace apparently has a museum and exhibitions of period furnishings, but I have not been able to visit due to significant delays in its completion, so I do not really know what is inside.

▲ Gedimino pilies bokštas (Upper Castle tower) and Pilies kalnas

The Upper Castle, situated on the hill (**Pilies kalnas**) above Cathedral Square, today consists mostly of one tower (**Gedimino pilies bokštas**). The top of the hill is accessible by way of a couple of paths, the easiest of which starts in the park next to Cathedral Square, and also by a funicular that starts at the National Museum. Gedimino pilies bokštas contains a small museum, but the best aspect of the tower is the viewing area at the top. I think the tower is well worth a visit, even if just for the view.

There is a small charge of about 3LTL for the funicular and a charge of about 5LTL for access to Gedimino pilies bokštas, though there is no charge to walk up the hill to the base of the tower. The tower museum and viewing area at the top of the tower are open every day during the summer and closed on Mondays from October through April.

▲ TV Tower

The TV tower is located outside the center of Vilnius, in a residential area of Soviet-era apartment blocks, and is not likely to be on your itinerary, but is worth noting. There is a restaurant and panoramic viewing area in the tower. The TV tower is an important site in Lithuania's struggle for independence, as this is the place where thirteen Lithuanians were killed by Soviets on January 13, 1991, some by being shot and some by being run over with tanks.[10] Crowds of people had turned out to protest and to protect the TV tower against seizure after Soviets had seized many other important buildings in the preceding days. There is a small memorial located at the tower for the Lithuanians killed there.

▲ Other Panoramic Viewing Spots

In addition to the TV Tower and the Upper Castle on Gedimi-nas Hill, there are a couple of other very good spots that provide panoramic views of Vilnius.

St. Johns' Bell Tower Observation Deck

The bell tower of St. Johns' church, the highest building in the Old Town at a height of about 45m (150 feet), is accessible to visitors and provides a great view. The tower is newly-renovated and now has an elevator for easier access to the ob-

---

[10] A fourteenth Lithuanian died of a heart attack at the scene, and is usually included in the list of Lithuanians who died as a result of Soviet actions.

servation deck. The bell tower can be entered either from the Grand Courtyard of Vilnius University or directly from Šv. Jono gatvė. The adult entrance fee is currently 5LTL, and will increase to 8LTL when a Museum of Science opens on the first floor. The bell tower is open from April through October, Tuesday through Saturday.

Skybar at Radisson Blu Hotel Lietuva

This bar provides one of the best views of Vilnius, and is worth a visit if you are looking for a good place to have a drink. This bar is located on the 22nd floor of the Radisson Blu Hotel Lietuva, a completely renovated hotel that actually dates back to Soviet times. The hotel is located on the opposite side of the Neris River (in the financial center) at Konstitucijos pr. 20, so it is likely worth taking a taxi to it. The bar's website is at www.sky-bar.lt.

▲ Neris River

The Neris winds its way through Vilnius, and provides a decent venue for a walk or run. Wide paths follow the river in both directions, providing an opportunity to see the low quality of Soviet concrete (watch out for the exposed rebar). A walk to the west (left) from the Old Town is the better direction, and will lead you to a nice open park on the opposite side of the river, which is a popular meeting spot for picnics and evening drinking.

▲ Green Bridge

This bridge that crosses the Neris river at Vilniaus g. is notable for the Soviet sculptures that adorn it. The four sculptures show workers and soldiers, and are some of the last Soviet sculptures remaining in place in any of the democratic former Soviet countries.

▲ Užupis

Užupis, or The Republic of Užupis (**Užupio Res Publika**), is an area of Vilnius just across the small Vilnia river to the east of the Old Town. Užupis was a long-neglected part of the city that attracted artists and other free spirits. The area has recently experienced significant gentrification but still retains many quirky characteristics. I recommend entering Užupis on Užupio g., just off Maironio g. This course takes you past the Užupis Republic sign, the mermaid (look down and to the left while on the bridge), and up to the angel statue, one of the most recognizable symbols of Užupis. Many cooperative art galleries exist down winding alleys, including a few to the left off Užupio g. near the river as you enter Užupis.

Angel statue in Užupis

The residents of Užupis declared "independence" in 1998, and established a constitution that is posted in many languages on a wall between Paupio g. 3 and 5 (take a right up the hill from the angel statue). This constitution consists of a list of rights and duties, some of which are tongue-in-cheek, while others are more serious. Examples include "Everyone has the right to die, but it is not a duty," "Everyone has a right to love," and "No one has the right to violence." My favorites are the cat-related rights: "Everyone has the right to love and take care of a cat" and "A cat is not obliged to love its master, but it must help him in difficult times." Perhaps as a result of these rights, I have found cats in Užupis to be some of the friendliest I have encountered in all of Europe.

If you take a left up the hill from the angel statue, you will reach Tores Restaurant on the left (across from a small park). This restaurant is worth the walk, less for the food than for the delicious house beers and for the great view of Vilnius from the patio (if the weather is good).

▲ Naujamiestis/Gedimino prospektas

The Naujamiestis (new city) lies to the west and south of the Senamiestis, with the boundary roughly at Pylimo g./Jogailos g. The most relevant part of the Naujamiestis for tourists is Gedimino prospektas, a wide boulevard stretching away from Cathedral Square to the west. Gedimino prospektas is lined with many fashionable shops and some restaurants, as well as a couple of casinos for the slot machine enthusiasts out there. A little more than halfway down Gedimino prospektas is the KGB Museum on the left, across the street from Lukiškių aikštė. At the far end of Gedimino prospektas are various government buildings, including the Seimas (Parliament) building that looks suspiciously like the Boston City Hall.

Restaurants and Bars

As I've written already, I think eating and drinking is one of the best ways to connect with Lithuania and Lithuanians. In consultation with our Lithuanian friends who are quite familiar with Vilnius restaurants and bars, below is a list of recommendations across the spectrum of choices. These are restaurants that are actually favorites of Lithuanians, not those that specifically target tourists.

I of course do urge you to try all of the unique Lithuanian dishes you can while in the country, which can be found at many restaurants, especially those in the areas most frequented by tourists, like Pilies gatvė, Rotušės aikštė, and Vokiečių gatvė.

You can find the restaurants, cafés, bars, and bakeries described below on the Vilnius Restaurants & Bars map available at www.experiencinglithuania.com.

Very Expensive
(by Lithuanian standards)

♦ *Domm* (in Vilnius City Hall)
Molecular gastronomy masterpieces
Didžioji g. 31
www.domm.lt
Tasting prix fixe menu: ~100-210LTL

♦ *La Provence*
French cuisine
Vokiečių g. 22
www.laprovence.lt
Main course: ~50-90LTL

♦ *Markus ir Ko.*
Steakhouse
Antokolskio g. 11 (off of Stiklių g.)
www.markusirko.lt
Main course: ~45-75LTL

Expensive-Average Prices
(in approximately decreasing order of prices)

♦ *La Pergola* (in Ghrotthus hotel)
International Cuisine
Ligoninės g. 7
www.grotthusshotel.com
Main course: ~30-50LTL

♦ *Saint Germain*
French country cuisine
Literatų g. 9
www.vynine.lt
Main course: ~30-50LTL

♦ *Zoe's Bar and Grill*
International cuisine
Odminių g. 3
www.zoesbargrill.com
Main course: ~20-50LTL

♦ *Balzac*
French Cuisine
Savičiaus g. 7
www.balzac.lt
Main course: ~30-50LTL

♦ *Bistro 18*
International Cuisine
Stiklių g. 18
www.bistro18.lt
Main course: ~25-40LTL

♦ *Rene*
Best mussels in town, good Belgian beer
Antokolskio g. 13
Main Course: ~20-35LTL

♦ *Tores*
Beautiful terrace in Užupis with great Vilnius old town views
and great house beer
Užupio g. 40
www.tores.lt
Main course: ~ 25-40LTL

♦ *Neringa*
One of the very few existing restaurants that also functioned
during Soviet times – used to be a gathering place for intellec-
tuals
Gedimino Ave. 23
www.restoranasneringa.lt
Main course: ~ 20-50LTL

♦ *Žemaičiai*
Upscale traditional Lithuanian food, with seating in a rustic
cellar or a cozy patio (in the summer).
Vokiečių g. 24
www.zemaiciai.lt
Main meat courses ~20-40LTL
Cepelinai - 18LTL for two or 9LTL for one

♦ *Kitchen*
European Cuisine
Didžioji g. 11
Main course: ~20-35LTL

♦ *Fiorentino*
Tuscan cuisine
Universiteto g. 4
www.fiorentino.lt
Main course: ~15-40LTL

♦ *Cozy*
Cozy Café
Dominikonų g. 10
www.cozy.lt
Main dishes 20-30 LTL

♦ *Brius Ly*
Asian Fusion
Islandijos g. 4
www.briusly.lt
Main course: ~15-20LTL

♦ *Jalta*
Local organic seasonal food. Farm to table.
70s Soviet Resort Interior Style.
Vykinto g. 17A
Main course: ~15-25LTL

Inexpensive

♦ *Gusto blyninė*
Crepes and European style pancakes.
Aušros vartų g. 6
www.gusto.lt
Main course: ~ 15LTL (pancakes less than that)

♦ *Picolo Canopi*
Small family restaurant, 5 tables. Great for home-style lasagna.
Bernardinų g. 10
Main course: ~10-20LTL

♦ *ŠMC (Contemporary Art Center) café*
Bohemian/intellectual crowd
Vokiečių g. 2

♦ *Sultininė*
Similar to Soviet style canteen, but serves decent cheap food
(including cepelinai)
Jogailos g. 6

Also, most bakeries usually have savory options, which can be a
great choice for inexpensive lunches (see under Baker-
ies/Pastries/Desserts).

Vegetarian restaurants

♦ *Vegafe* (In Yoga Center)
Vegetarian café and natural juice bar
Augustijonų g. 2
Main course: ~15LTL

♦ *Mano Guru*
Great for salad lovers
Vilniaus g. 22/Labdarių g. 1
www.manoguru.lt

♦ *Raw Raw*
Raw vegetarian food
www.rawraw.lt
Skapo g. 10
Main course: ~10-20LTL

Bakeries/Pastries/Desserts

♦ *Thierry kepykla*
Great little French bakery in Užupis. Best for croissants
Užupio g. 19

♦ *Cukatos*
Homemade, natural ingredients bakery; can find egg-free, dairy-free, gluten-free products
Trakų g. 16
www.cukatos.lt

♦ *Pilies kepyklėlė*
Nice bakery serving fresh pastries and baked goods. Best for desserts.
Pilies g. 19
You can also order regular inexpensive lunches

♦ *Kibin inn*
Bakery, Pastries, Savory pastries (Kibins)
Vilniaus g. 21
Kibins ~ 7LTL

♦ *Tie Kepėjai*
Fresh baked organic cupcakes, macarons, Lithuanian marshmallows and other sweets in a cozy atmosphere
Tilto g. 6
www.kepejai.lt

Wine bars
(Recently increasingly fashionable
Wine/Mediterranean style places)

♦ *Notre vie*
Stiklių g. 10
www.notrevie.lt

♦ *Tappo d'oro*
L. Stuokos-Gucevičiaus g. 7/ Vokiečių g. 8

♦ *In Vino*
Aušros vartų g. 7
www.invino.lt

Bars

♦ *Piano Man Bar*
Islandijos g. 1
Pub with pub quiz tournaments in English every Monday

♦ *Paparazzi bar*
Totorių g. 3
www.paparazzi.lt

♦ *Soul Box*
Good cocktails
Vilniaus g. 23
www.soulbox.lt

♦ *Skybar* (Radisson Blu Hotel, 22nd floor)
Great Vilnius center views, cozy atmosphere
Konstitucijos pr. 20
www.sky-bar.lt

♦ *Portobello Bar* (next door to In Vino)
Great beer
Aušros vartų g. 7

♦ *Nino bar*
(Cozy Café cellar)
Dominikonų 10

Vilnius Vicinity

You can find the locations of all of the sites mentioned in this section on the Map of Other Places Mentioned in the Guide at www.experiencinglithuania.com.

Two of Lithuania's early capitals, Trakai and Kernavė, are located within about 40km of Vilnius. Directly to the west, Trakai is situated in a picturesque lake area. Northwest of Vilnius, and north of Trakai, Kernavė is located near the Neris river.

Trakai

Trakai Island Castle

Trakai is an especially popular tourist destination, with historical wooden houses of the local Karaites surrounded by lakes. The main attraction of the town is the restored castle on an island in Lake Galvė. The island castle dates from around 1400, and was constructed during the time of Vytautas the Great. Although significant portions of the castle are original, it has also undergone substantial restoration throughout the latter half of the 20th century. The castle can be toured for a fee, and provides some great historical expositions (along with some oddball collections that aren't very related to the history of the castle). I think the tour and expositions are worth the fee. You can also take rowboats and pedal boats out onto the lake for a nice tour around the island.

A flashy multimedia site for the Trakai Castle is available at www.trakaimuziejus.lt. The castle is open every day of the week May through September, and closed Mondays October through April. Admission to the castle is 14LTL for adults.

While in Trakai, visitors should take the opportunity to have a lunch of **kibinai** prepared by the local Karaites. The Karaites (also known as Karaims) are an ethnic group of Turkic people, originally from the Crimean region, who practice a form of Judaism. The Karaites in Trakai are descendants of families brought by Vytautas to Trakai in the late 14th century after he defeated the Tartars in 1392. Karaites were used as bodyguards and provided castle security for centuries. The Karaite population in Lithuania was decimated in the 17th and 18th centuries due to wars, plague and famine in the region. Today, a few hundred Karaite live in the area.

Interestingly, in the 19th century, the Karaites successfully petitioned Tsarist Russia (the occupier at the time) to legally recognize them as a Turkic ethnicity, not a Jewish ethnicity, which enhanced their rights. Later, in 1934, based on the legal status they had attained under Russian rule, the Karaites also gained from the German government exemption from Jewish laws.[11]

---

[11] I have not been able to determine why the Karaims were dealing with the German government, because Trakai was at that time in territory controlled by Poland.

Ultimately, this appears to have saved them from the genocide that befell the rest of the Jewish population of Lithuania.

Kernavė

Kernavė is a very small town in the vicinity of one of the early capitals of Lithuania, and the archeological site there has been placed on the UNESCO World Heritage list. A visit to Kernavė is a good add-on to a day trip out to Trakai, as they combine to take you through the history of early Lithuania (and neither location necessitates a full day of exploring on its own). The Kernavė Cultural Reserve includes an area that had settlements for millennia, including many settlements in the valley along the nearby Neris river. These settlements have been the site of many archeological discoveries, most of which are now housed in the Archeological and Historical Museum, located in the town, which should be re-opening in the near future.

During the early Middle Ages, Baltic peoples formed protective hillforts on mounds to provide fortified locations for settlement and defense. Kernavė features five of these mounds, and it was perhaps the most significant hillfort complex in all of the Baltics. It is believed by some that Mindaugas' crowning as King of Lithuania in 1253 may have occurred at Kernavė. The town and castle were destroyed in 1390 during a civil war, and Kernavė was never again a seat of power in Lithuania.

Kernavė is also the site of the biggest Midsummer's Eve celebration in Lithuania. This traditional pagan celebration (Midsummer's Eve) has been joined with the Christian day for John to be the celebration known as **Joninės**, and takes place on June 24 each year. On that day, the town erupts into a massive frenzy of festivities, replete with plenty of fires. As it is their name day, people with names derived from John (**Jonas** and **Janina**) (and others who want to feel special) adorn their heads with wreaths made of oak leaves, branches, and flowers. After midnight, everyone treks down to the river to release the wreaths into the current for good luck.

The website for the Kernavė Cultural Reserve is at www.kernave.org. The area itself is always open and can be walked about with no charge. The archeological museum is scheduled to re-open in May of 2012. Opening times and prices are not yet posted.

Green Lakes

If you are in Vilnius and are interested in getting out into nature near the city, the Green Lakes area in the Verkiai Regional Park provides a great venue for swimming and walking/running/biking through the forests. This is one of the places that locals know and love, but few visitors to Lithuania ever make it there.

To get to the best swimming access for the Green Lakes at Balsys ežeras (Balsys Lake), take the A14 north from Vilnius for about 6.5km (from the Ukmergės gatvė bridge), turn right onto Mokslininkų gatvė/Molėtų plentas, go through the roundabout onto Žaliujų ežerų gatvė, follow this road for about 5km, then take a left toward the lake at the last road before you reach a large sodai community. The swimming area is a short drive up this road. The exact location is shown on the Map of Other Places Mentioned in the Guide available online at www.experiencinglithuania.com.

Europos parkas

I include this in the guide simply to recommend against going to this sculpture park located near the "Center of Europe" outside of Vilnius. There's nothing terrible about it, but unless you absolutely adore installation art, the entry price (25LTL) plus substantial parking fee (not disclosed on the website) plus fee to take pictures (not disclosed on the website) and overpriced restaurant (high prices not disclosed on the website) are not worth it.

Shopping Malls

If you find yourself needing something from a specialized shop, or otherwise just crave the shopping mall (**prekybos centras**) experience, there are a number of shopping malls located in and around Vilnius. The best mall overall is the Akropolis, located on Ozo gatvė just off of the A2 and the A14, about a 5km drive north of the Old Town. This large shopping mall even contains an ice rink, bowling alley, movie theater, and grocery store. Another mall, Ozas, is located near the Akropolis, but I don't really recommend it, as it seems mostly to be second-tier shops. The Europa mall is a rather high-end shopping mall located in the Šnipiškės/financial district on the other side of the Neris river from the Old Town. Another fairly high-end mall, Gedimino 9, is located on Gedimino prospektas.

VCUP, the first Western style mall to be developed after the restoration of independence is also located in Šnipiškės (and easily seen from the Old Town). This mall is interesting because during Soviet times it was actually the **Vilniaus Centrinė Universalinė Parduotuvė** (VCUP) – essentially a Soviet department store – that carried a variety of goods. These shopping centers were common throughout the Soviet Union. Today, this mall is a bit lower-end than the other malls and has an oddball mix of Lithuanian/European shops you've probably never heard of.

Kaunas

(Population: approx. 360,000)

Old Town of Kaunas and the confluence of the Nemunas and Neris rivers

Although Kaunas is somewhat less cosmopolitan than Vilnius, it is actually a thriving city with a great deal of charm and it tends to not get the respect or attention that it deserves. While Vilnius has grown into the financial and cultural center of Lithuania, Kaunas, which is the second largest city in the country, remains a quieter city with its economy based more on industry and distribution. However, the central area of Kaunas presents a good opportunity for visitors to explore more of Lithuania's history and enjoy a welcoming and entertaining environment.

Many Lithuanians actually regard Kaunas as the most "Lithuanian" city of the country. Vilnius has had tremendous population shifts that at some points have left ethnic Lithuanians as a very small minority, while Kaunas has had a more stable ethnic Lithuanian population over time. Vilnius has a relatively diverse population today, while Kaunas is approximately 92% Lithuanian. In addition, during most of Lithuania's independence in the 1920s-30s, Kaunas served as the capital of the country because Vilnius was under the control of Poland. Furthermore, during Soviet times, Kaunas had less of a Russian presence than Vilnius, and Kaunas had a stronger contingent of anti-Soviet activity. In the 1980s, the successful Kaunas basketball team Žalgiris also embodied a significant amount of Lithuanian national pride, acting in a sense as the national team.

The recently improved main tourism website for Kaunas is located at http://visit.kaunas.lt. Tourism offices operate at the airport (when Ryanair flights arrive), in the bus station, in the train station, and in the Park Inn Hotel at K. Donelaičio gatvė 27 (located just off of Laisvės alėja near the Soboras church (see below)).

Sites

You can find the locations of the churches, museums, and other sites described below on the Kaunas Places of Interest map at www.experiencinglithuania.com.

▲ Laisvės alėja and Vilniaus gatvė

The main area for visitors to Kaunas stretches from the grand Church of St. Michael the Archangel (originally a Russian Orthodox church and today a Catholic church), also known as the "Soboras" church, directly west along Laisvės alėja and down Vilniaus gatvė to the Rotušės aikštė (Town Hall Square). Laisvės alėja is a grand pedestrian boulevard that is full of shops and cafés.[12] This might also be a good location for you to

---

[12] Amazingly, Laisvės alėja has, within the span of about ten years, experienced the ups and downs experienced by some American downtowns: It was revitalized and thriving, then a shopping mall opened in another part of town, leading to an exodus

93

witness a style phenomenon somewhat unique to Kaunas. It is not uncommon to see girls known as "fifos" or "kavianskos" who have dyed jet black or bleach blond hair, wear lots of eye makeup and dress rather provocatively.

Laisvės alėja leads directly into Vilniaus gatvė, which proceeds through the heart of the small old town (senamiestis). The old town is squeezed into the area where the Neris River (to the north) and Nemunas River (to the south) meet. This area has been mostly renovated from its significantly degenerated state during Soviet times. Vilniaus gatvė will deliver a visitor to the vibrant Rotušės aikštė.

▲ Rotušės Aikštė and Surrounding Area

The Rotušės aikštė is surrounded by restaurants, shops, and small museums, and features the picturesque Rotušė (Town Hall) and Kauno Šv. Pranciškaus Ksavero (St. Francis Xavier) church. The square is often bustling with activity during warm summer evenings and is the central location for many celebrations. We've had a wild time dancing inside the square's giant artificial Christmas tree during the New Year's celebration!

Kitty corner to the square, with its entrance on Aleksoto gatvė, is the impressive Cathedral of Saints Peter and Paul, the largest Gothic church in Lithuania, which dates back to the early 15th century. Farther down Aleksoto gatvė to the south (toward the Nemunas) is the small but remarkable Perkūnas House (Perkūno namas). Dating to the late 15th century, this red brick building exhibits some elaborate brickwork very reminiscent of St. Anne's church in Vilnius. A little farther down the street, very near the river, is the red brick Gothic Vytautas the Great

---

of businesses, and now Laisvės alėja is enjoying another revitalization and is thriving again.

Church, which originally dates back to 1400, but has had significant renovations.

Some of the best restaurants are located in the area around Vilniaus gatvė and the Rotušės aikštė (recommended restaurants are listed below in the next section). The Daugirdas Restaurant, located in the Daugirdas Hotel on T. Daugirdo gatvė, is highly recommended for international cuisine. The proprietors also have a nice outdoor café area just down the street along the Nemunas river called Daugirdo Uostas. There is also an interesting bar just off the square on Muitinės gatvė called Gyvas Alus, which serves and sells "live" beer.

Old Town of Kaunas

▲ Kaunas Castle

A walk past the Rotušės aikštė will lead you to a nice park at the confluence of the Nemunas and Neris Rivers. The remains of the Kaunas Castle (**Kauno Pilis**), parts of which were originally built in the 14th century and which was the site of many contentious battles between Lithuanians and Teutonic Knights, are located in the park. The castle is currently undergoing major renovations.

▲ Museums Near Vienybės aikštė

Three notable museums are clustered on V. Putvinskio gatvė and K. Donelaičio gatvė, situated in the vicinity of another square, Vienybės aikštė, just north of Laisvės alėja.

The **Vytautas the Great War Museum**, located at K. Donelaičio g. 64, is an interesting museum documenting the history of warfare as it relates to Lithuania, especially armament. The museum also contains the wreckage of the famous plane, *Lituanica*, which was flown non-stop across the Atlantic by two Lithuanian-Americans in 1933, but tragically crashed about 775km (480 mi.) short of their destination, Kaunas. The museum itself does not have an English language website, which does not surprise me, because when I visited a few years ago very few of the displays provided information in English either. Fortunately, the Lithuanian museum website at www.muziejai.lt provides good details about the museum. Admission is 4LTL. The museum is closed Mondays from April to September and closed Sundays and Mondays from October to March.

Located in the same building as the War Museum but with the entrance on the opposite side, at V. Putvinskio g. 55, the **M. K. Čiurlionis State Art Museum** contains the vast majority of the paintings by Mikalojus Konstantinas Čiurlionis. Čiurlionis is best known for dreamy symbolic paintings that often evoke musical themes, as he was also an accomplished composer. The museum also displays some folk art in a separate area. The museum is closed on Mondays, and admission is 6LTL. The museum's official website is www.ciurlionis.lt, but the

Lithuanian museum site at www.muziejai.lt may be more helpful.

The quirky **Devils' Museum**, located at V. Putvinskio g. 64 across from the Čiurlionis Museum, houses thousands of representations of the Devil, along with other mythical creatures. The wide variety of figures, many of which are humorous, is quite amusing. The museum also contains some of the art created by the museum's founder, Antanas Žmuidzinavičius. Admission is 6LTL and the museum is closed Mondays. The Lithuanian museum website www.muziejai.lt provides the best information about the museum.

▲ Akropolis Shopping Mall

Three blocks south from the "Soboras" church is the large Akropolis shopping mall, which displays interesting architectural features because it was constructed incorporating some of the buildings existing at the location. This mall includes a bowling alley, movie theater and grocery store. The Žalgiris Arena is located right across from the Akropolis on a small island accessible by bridge.

▲ Stumbras Museum

A short walk east of the Akropolis mall, fairly near the train station, is the Stumbras factory and museum, located at K. Būgos gatvė 7. The museum, which covers the history and present-day production of the distillery, is open by appointment for groups of five or more, and the guided tour can be accompanied by tastings. Tours can be arranged online at http://stumbras.eu/museum.

Restaurants and Bars

Below is a list of bars and restaurants in Kaunas, recommended by our Lithuanian friends and family. Note that prices in Kaunas restaurants are generally lower than in Vilnius.

You can find the locations of all of the restaurants and bars listed below on the Kaunas Restaurants & Bars map available at www.experiencinglithuania.com.

Relatively Expensive

♦ *Daugirdas*
Gothic cellars, fireplace in a beautifully restored Kaunas old town hotel
T. Daugirdo g. 4
Main course: ~25-50LTL
www.daugirdas.lt/en/restaurant

♦ *Senieji rūsiai (Old Cellars)*
Another restaurant in beautiful restored 17th century cellars
Vilniaus g. 34
Main course: ~30-55LTL
www.seniejirusiai.lt/en/

♦ *Sadutė*
Located in one of the oldest buildings in Kaunas – serves European cuisine. Has expansive outdoor seating right in the Rotušės aikštė during the summer.
Rotušės aikštė 4
Main course: ~20-40LTL
www.sadute.lt

Average prices

♦ *Pizza Jazz*
Close to the fountain in the center of Laisvės alėja. Trendy decor, trendy menu.
Laisvės alėja 68
Main course: ~20-30LTL
www.pj.lt

♦ *Medžiotojų užeiga*
Best place in Kaunas to try game meat.
Rotušės aikštė 10
Main course: ~25-45LTL
www.medziotojai.lt

♦ *Buon Giorno Taverna* (Vilniaus g. 34)
& *Buon Giorno Trattoria* (Daukanto g. 14)
Recently opened Italian restaurants and wine bars, popular hangout places for locals.
www.buongiorno.lt

♦ *Avilys*
Yet another restaurant in a cozy cellar with its own brewery (try their honey beer).
Main Course: ~25-40LTL
Vilniaus g. 34

Relatively Inexpensive

♦ *Bajorkiemis „City"*
Non-touristy option for good traditional Lithuanian food served in a modern environment
Kęstučio g. 86 / I. Kanto g. 18
Main Course: ~10-20LTL
www.bajorkiemis.lt

♦ *Bernelių užeiga*
This is a slightly more touristy option for traditional Lithuanian food (including waiters and waitresses dressed in traditional Lithuanian costumes). Two locations of this restaurant book-end the main pedestrian area of Kaunas, with one located at K. Donelaičio g. 11, near the Soboras church, and one at M. Valančiaus g. 9, near the Rotušės aikštė. Another restaurant is located in the Akropolis mall.
Main Course: ~10-20LTL
www.berneliuuzeiga.eu

♦ *Flamenco*
Coffee, Wine and Spanish Tapas bar
Laisvės alėja 74

♦ *Piano Piano*
One of the recently opened fashionable wine bars increasingly popular with locals.
Rotušės aikštė 4

Kaunas Vicinity

You can find all of the sites mentioned in this section on the Map of Other Places Mentioned in the Guide available at www.experiencinglithuania.com.

Ninth Fort Museum
The Ninth Fort site, topped with a striking memorial sculpture, is a very powerful place to visit. This has been the site of tremendous suffering by many nationalities at the hands of whichever occupier was in power at the time. The fort, and another building built as a museum, now explore the history of the place and memorialize the events that happened there. It is also

one of the few places in Lithuania that strikes me as giving sufficiently comprehensive coverage of the Holocaust events that occurred in the country.

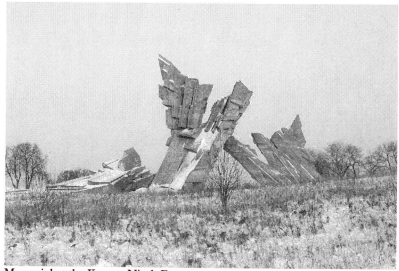

Memorial at the Kaunas Ninth Fort

The Ninth Fort, completed in 1911, was an integral part of the stationary defenses of Kaunas known as the Kaunas Fortress (nine forts and nine gun batteries surrounding the city), and also served as a notorious prison for many periods of its use. The forts comprising the Kaunas Fortress were built by the Russian rulers in the late 19th and early 20th centuries, and were later used by the independent state of Lithuania.

The Ninth Fort was used to imprison and kill Lithuanians targeted by the Soviets after they invaded in 1940. When the Nazis invaded in 1941, they took over the fort and used it as one of the primary locations for imprisoning and killing Jews from Kaunas, other parts of Lithuania, and even France.

The Occupation Museum, the first part of the tour, focuses primarily on the Soviet and Nazi atrocities committed against ethnic Lithuanians. The museum features photographs and historical artifacts, as well as a lot of art pieces related to the Soviet occupation. The museum also includes an interesting exposition about Romas Kalanta, the university student who set himself on fire on Laisvės alėja in Kaunas in 1972 to protest Soviet policies.

The Fortress Museum, inside the fort itself, has information about the history of the fort and focuses primarily on the mass killing of Jews there and throughout Lithuania during the Nazi occupation. The museum has good displays in English spread out among many rooms on multiple floors, including information about the "Great Action" of October 28-29, 1941 and the "Children's Action" of March 27, 1944. Another exhibition focuses on Chiune Sugihara, the Japanese diplomat who worked tirelessly to issue transit visas to Jews from Lithuania and Poland, thereby saving the lives of thousands. (There is also a small museum in Kaunas dedicated to Chiune Sugihara. Information is available at www.sugiharahouse.lt.)

Note that it is extremely cold and fairly damp in the fort. Even on one of the hottest days I ever experienced in Lithuania it was so cold that the museum staff were wearing heavy down coats.

The Ninth Fort is located just inside the city limits of Kaunas, to the north of the city itself, but requires a car or bus trip. Visitors arriving at the fort should be forewarned that there is essentially no signage and it can be a little tricky to get to. (Our Garmin GPS was not able to get us to the entrance correctly.) Access to the fort is from the A5, right near the intersection with the A1. The entrance off the A5 is just a small road past a gas station. Once parked, walk to the far right end of the new building to get to the entrance.

The website for the fort is located at www.9fortomuziejus.lt, but unfortunately it is not available in English. The Museums of Lithuania website has information available at www.muziejai.lt. Admission is 5LTL for adults and there is an additional fee for an optional guided tour through the ramparts. The museum is closed on Tuesdays year round and closed on Mondays November through March, but the grounds are always open.

Pažaislis Monastery

The Pažaislis Monastery is located on the eastern edge of the municipality of Kaunas on a peninsula jutting out into the Kaunas Sea (a large reservoir). The monastery was founded in 1664 for monks of the Camaldolese order, with the Church of the Visitation consecrated in 1674. The monastery has had a tumultuous history, being substantially desecrated by Napoleon's troops in 1812, then closed by Russian authorities in 1832 and transferred to Russian Orthodox control. When the Russians left in 1914, they stripped the monastery of its valuables. After use as a hospital by the Germans in WWI, the monastery was transferred to the Sisters of St. Casimir. The Soviets expelled the Sisters in 1948, and used the monastery for various purposes during the period of occupation. The monastery was returned to the Sisters in 1992 after the restoration of independence.

Pažaislis Monastery

The monastery and church are Baroque structures comprising a very orderly complex. The complex is centered on the Church of the Visitation of the Virgin Mary to Elizabeth, an impressive structure with a facade of two towers and a large dome behind. The interior of the church boasts stucco mouldings, frescoes, and a couple of historical paintings, including The Mother of Beautiful Love.

The monastery is located east of Kaunas, just off T. Masiulio gatvė. If arriving from Vilnius, take the first Kaunas exit off the A1 and continue on Ateities plentas until it turns into T. Masiulio gatvė. The monastery is open for tours Tuesday through Saturday. Tickets are 10LTL. Additional information about the monastery can be found at http://pazaislis.org.

Rumšiškės

Rumšiškės is an "open-air ethnographic museum" located about 20km east of Kaunas, just off the A1. This sprawling complex was developed to showcase the traditional rural lifestyle of Lithuanians of the 18th and 19th centuries. Many traditional homestead buildings have been moved to and reassembled on the site, and a traditional town center has also been recreated. The town center houses a number of traditional workshops, including a blacksmith, metalworker, and weaver. Strangely, I once walked into the weaving shop to find a nice old lady weaving away while listening to Guns N' Roses – I believe it was "Welcome to the Jungle." The museum is organized to showcase the types of homesteads throughout the four main ethnographic regions of the country. The museum has also expanded to include exhibits about the conditions of Lithuanians deported to Siberia.

A wide variety of events, including many elaborate holiday celebrations, occur at the museum throughout the year. The biggest event of the year is Shrove Tuesday (**Užgavėnės**) also known as Mardi Gras, which includes the burning of an effigy symbolizing winter, a battle staged between costumed actors portraying Spring and Winter, plenty of devils and witches, and the consumption of pancakes (**blynai**).

Information about the museum is available at www.llbm.lt. Opening hours are a little complicated. The museum (including exhibitions inside the buildings) is open 10am to 6pm Wednesday through Sunday, May through September. During the rest of the year, the museum is open similar hours, but only for walking around. Admission ranges up to 10LTL per person.

Klaipėda

(Population: approx. 180,000)

Inner courtyard in Klaipėda's Old Town

Klaipėda is Lithuania's critical port city, and is worth a short visit on your way to one of the coastal resort towns. It is also likely to be of interest to Germans or their descendants, as it was for a long time a German city with a majority German population.

The Teutonic Knights established a castle at present-day Klaipėda in 1252, founding Memelburg, later shortened to Memel. The city grew and flourished as a part of Livonia and Prussia, and later as part of the unified German Empire. After the defeat of Germany in WWI, the city was stripped from Germany and became a protectorate of the Entente States with a French garrison. Before the fate of the city could be decided by the League of Nations, Lithuanians fomented an uprising in

1923 that resulted in the annexation of the city by the newly independent Lithuania. Nazi Germany invaded the city in 1939 and the USSR took over in 1945.

Today, Klaipėda has an interesting, if small, old town. The city was significantly destroyed during WWII, as it was a strategic location held by the Germans, but retains some nice historical buildings in the area bounded approximately by the Danės River, Pilies gatvė, Turgaus aikštė (not gatvė) and the old fort.

The Švyturys brewery is located in Klaipėda, which would be an interesting attraction to visit if you can squeeze into their not very convenient schedule. Tours of the brewery need to be scheduled in advance, and are available Monday through Friday between 10am and 3pm. The English language tour costs 150LTL for up to 5 people, and 30LTL for each person more than 5. Tours can be arranged at the tourism office or by email or phone. Information about Švyturys and contact information for the brewery can be found at www.svyturys.lt.

Information about visiting Klaipėda can be found at www.klaipedainfo.lt. The tourism office is located at Turgaus gatvė 7, right in the heart of the old town.

Druskininkai

Druskonis lake in Druskininkai

Druskininkai is a picturesque spa town located in the southern part of Lithuania, very close to the borders with Belarus and Poland. The small town is nestled in a bend of the Nemunas River and surrounded by vast pine forests, which contribute to the clear, fresh air for which it is known. Many paths meander through the forests, and around the lakes and river, allowing for a relaxed enjoyment of nature. The town is also filled with spa facilities, providing many opportunities for healthy relaxation.

The town has long been known for its mineral waters (**druska** means "salt") and healthy air, and began to be developed as a holiday destination in the 18th century. In 1837, Czar Nicholas I of Russia officially designated it a spa town, leading to increased development of the resort. Druskininkai developed further into a very popular resort town during the period of Soviet occupation.

Today, after a period of decline following independence, the town is enjoying a significant revival as a destination for Lithuanians, Poles, Russians, and other vacationers. Many spas and hotels have been renovated, and there is seemingly constant development, construction, and infrastructure renovation, partly because the town has been the recipient of a significant amount of EU funding. Just within the last year, major portions of the parks have been revitalized, a large bridge across the Nemunas has been opened, significant road and sidewalk improvements have been made, the beach and swimming facilities were expanded, and a new indoor/outdoor downhill skiing area has opened.

The heart of the town (for tourists at least) consists of the area around Vilniaus alėja, which runs from the Vandens Parkas (Aqua Park) on one end to the main Druskininkai church on the other, along with the waterfront of the lake just across the street.

Druskininkai is known for a quaint, decorative architectural style of buildings from its early days as a resort town. The streets to the west of Vilniaus alėja (away from the river) are filled with colorful examples of this style. In the center of Laisvės aikštė is an impressive blue Russian Orthodox church. There is also a hodgepodge of Soviet era buildings in town, some of which, including the Pušynas Hotel and the Vandens Parkas, exhibit interesting and not unpleasant architectural design features. Others, such as the Nemunas Hotel, a vacant monstrosity to the west of Laisvės aikštė, demonstrate the worst of Soviet era architecture.[13]

---

[13] The rumors are that this building, although it is ugly and out of place, is slated to be renovated as part of a massive development on the surrounding site. Apparently the height of the building is grandfathered in, so it is to a developer's advantage to keep it.

Pušynas Hotel - an example of interesting Soviet architecture

Druskininkai is also well-known as the location where Mikalojus Konstantinas Čiurlionis, a famous Lithuanian painter and composer, lived for much of his working life during the first decade of the 20th century. Čiurlionis' paintings often contained musical themes, and his works greatly affected Lithuanian culture in the early 20th century. There are a couple of small Čiurlionis museums in Druskininkai, but the majority of his work is housed in Kaunas.

Plenty of information about Druskininkai is available at the Druskininkai tourism website (http://info.druskininkai.lt). (This site, as is the case with many Lithuanian sites, has some amusingly terrible English.) Tourism offices are located at M. K. Čiurlionio gatvė 65 (about a block down from the main church, across from the small Maxima) and at the camping center on Gardino gatvė.

You can find all of the sites, spas, restaurants, and activities mentioned in this section on the Druskininkai Places of Interest map at www.experiencinglithuania.com.

Below are descriptions of some of the various activities available to visitors:

Bicycling/Walking/Running

Druskininkai is made for getting outside and exercising or leisurely touring, with its many paths winding around town, by the river and lakes, and out into the forests. Bike rentals are available at a few places, including quite a few on Vilniaus gatvė and at the Europa Royale Hotel. Signs are posted that can direct you through the many forest paths. The best paths can be accessed starting on Turistų gatvė, next to Druskonis lake. Should you feel a little daring, you can bike all the way to the Belarus border without too much effort. A very nice map of the trails is available at http://info.druskininkai.lt.

Swimming

If it is warm enough, you can swim in the Vijūnėlė pond, where there is a sandy beach. This small lake is just past Druskonis lake along the new walkways to the right of Turistų gatvė. The beach has recently been significantly expanded, and changing facilities and bathrooms have been built at the location.

While on the subject, I should note that Lithuanian men generally don't wear the Speedo type bathing suits that Americans think all Europeans wear. They actually often wear shorts that, while smaller and tighter fitting than the surfer shorts that are popular in the U.S., are much more modest than "banana hammocks."

Snow Arena

The Snow Arena is an indoor/outdoor year round downhill skiing facility that, after multiple construction delays, finally opened in August of 2011. Located a couple of kilometers across the Nemunas from Druskininkai, this is an exciting addition to the attractions in the area, especially since downhill skiing is extremely limited in Lithuania. This facility was opened as the Snoras Snow Arena, but the "Snoras" was dropped after the Lithuanian government seized Snoras Bank in November of 2011 under suspicion of significant fraud and embezzlement by the bank's owners.

Ski rentals and tickets for periods as short as an hour or two are available. Information is available at www.snowarena.lt.

Aqua Park/Vandens Parkas

This indoor water park is a very fun highlight of Druskininkai. The water park is set within a renovated spa complex from Soviet times, and retains some interesting design and architectural elements.

The water park is split into two connected areas – a family area and an adults only area (the "Alita Bath Complex"). The family area has a wide mix of the usual indoor water park attractions – various water slides (including the surprisingly extreme *Ekstremalusis* – seriously guys, keep your legs together or your wedding tackle is in for a painful surprise at the end), hot tubs, a big pool, a wave pool, a lazy river, a sun room, a couple of saunas, and some kids' play areas. This area is worth spending some time in for the water slides, wave pool and lazy river.

The real fun is in the adults only area, which, although the management does like to remind visitors that clothing is optional, really doesn't have much "adult" about it.[14] This area includes something on the order of 15 steam rooms and 15 (dry) saunas, each with different temperatures and humidity levels. There are also hot tubs and a big pool, complete with a swim-up bar for a little light refreshment. An outdoor area also includes a hot tub, pool and a couple of saunas.

The water park offers a schedule of "programmes" throughout the day in different saunas, such as salt and honey scrubs in the steam rooms, and extreme heat and birch branch beating sessions in the dry saunas. I much prefer the dry saunas to the steam rooms, but the programmes in the steam rooms can be enjoyable and good for the skin. These scheduled programmes are complimentary, but some of the scrubs can also be purchased for a small fee at other times.

I recommend that newcomers experiment with the different types of saunas and steam rooms, moving gradually up in temperature. Once you've acclimated, I suggest you find one of the hottest dry saunas, named "Tilia" (near the café on the third floor), work up a sweat, then make use of the ice chamber or cold tub just outside the sauna. The ice chamber is a delightfully cold space where you can dump cold water over your head or toss ice chips at one another. You can find another of the hottest dry saunas (both have a target temperature of 90°C (194°F)), along with a cold-water bucket, in the outdoor area.

Admission to the water park can be purchased for 1, 2, 3, or 4 hours, or all day. For a first visit, I recommend at least 4 hours, which only costs a little less than the whole day, so why not go

---

[14] I've rarely seen anyone nude in this area, but it does happen occasionally, especially in connection with the birch branch beatings in saunas. Apparently the last Friday evening of each month is dedicated to nudists.

all the way? You will get a wristband that serves as your ticket and also as a way to pay for anything in the park, including for food and beverages, which you'll probably need to buy since you can't leave and return within the time you've purchased.

I do recommend that you bring bottles of water (you're gonna need it!) and a towel or two. Two towels is best so you can have one normal, dryin' towel and one sweatin' towel. Proper sauna etiquette is that in the dry sauna you should lay a towel down below you – if sitting, it should be both under your butt and under your feet. Towels and robes can also be rented (with your wristband) from a kiosk in the locker room.

Be aware that the changing/locker room situation can be a bit confusing: you enter into a small changing room, put down the bench to close yourself in, change, then put the bench up and pass into a unisex locker room through the other door of the changing room. You exit through the same changing spaces. Another word of caution: <u>be very careful walking on the wet floors throughout the water park</u>, as they are quite slippery and do not have the sort of non-slip coating you would find in a more litigious country. I recommend that you bring flip-flops if possible. There are also a couple of places where the floor is uneven (mostly at the entrances to bathrooms or locker rooms) that warrant your close attention.

Information can be found at www.akvapark.lt.

Spas

Druskininkai offers a wide range of spa services, which vary from basic to luxurious. The normal services of facials, massages, etc. are widely available, and some facilities provide some adventurous options. For instance, I've tried a turpentine bath,

114

which essentially smelled like pine water. Whatever you choose, prices are very reasonable compared to prices for comparable services in the U.S. English abilities of the staff vary, with front office personnel usually speaking English well, but some of the service providers speaking little to no English. Tipping is generally not expected in connection with spa services.

I recommend the East Island Spa (www.east-island.lt), located in the same building as the Aqua Park. The service at this spa is probably the most similar to spas that you might visit in North America or Western Europe, although that does come with prices that approach those that you would expect in those spas. You can take the opportunity to try the kangal fish – tiny fish that nibble off dead skin from your feet and other parts of your body. (Though be aware that these are not legal in some U.S. states due to health concerns.) This spa can be accessed both from within and from outside of the water park. If you enter from the water park, you will not be using up the time you have paid for in the park because you will "clock out" from the park.

I also recommend SPA Vilnius (www.spa-vilnius.lt), which is probably the best-known spa in Druskininkai. This spa is quite a bit larger than East Island and provides excellent service. Navigating the spa can be a bit confusing, but there are plenty of English speaking staff to help.

I will also mention another spa, Druskininkų Gydykla (www.gydykla.lt), which is worth trying if you are interested in a little more traditional Druskinkinkai spa service. This spa is housed in one of the oldest facilities, renovated in 2002-03, and offers a variety of services in a manner closer to those provided during Soviet times. Prices are also a bit lower than the other two spas recommended above. Even if you do not visit for spa services, I recommend you stop by for a taste of the various mineral waters on tap, available for a nominal charge in the lobby area. You really shouldn't leave Druskininkai without tasting some warm, salty water. It's... an experience.

Sports

Druskininkai is growing its options for sports recreation as tourism increases. Sūkurys (www.sukurys.lt) has some very nice clay tennis courts, as well as bowling and billiards. A bowling alley is also located at the Aqua Park. If you like volleyball, new beach volleyball courts have been set up near the beach of the Vijūnėlės pond.

ONE Adventure Park

This adventure park, which consists mostly of an elaborate ropes course and zip-lines, is located just across the street from the Vandens Parkas, near the Nemunas River. I have not tried this yet, but it certainly looks like fun. Information is available at www.onenuotykiuparkas.lt.

Souvenirs/Shopping

There are a number of souvenir and jewelry shops in town, including in the water park and on the main streets. I highly recommend the art shop Sofa (Galerija "Sofa") located on Vilniaus gatvė (the pedestrian walkway). This shop sells unique and fanciful artworks, most of which are made by artists from the region. There is also a very nice amber and jewelry shop next door.

If you are looking for inexpensive souvenirs, there are often vendors lined up outside near the Europa Royale Hotel and the Druskininkų Gydykla.

Restaurants

Below are our favorite restaurants in Druskininkai, listed in order of our preference. Prices are generally relatively inexpensive – much lower than prices in Vilnius.

♦ *Sicilija*

Great, inexpensive restaurant. While it may be categorized as a pizza place, it makes good Lithuanian food at great prices. It can be quite crowded, especially if the patio is not open. Try their doughnuts (**spurgos**) with chocolate sauce. This is our favorite place to eat in Druskininkai.
Taikos g. 9
Main Courses: ~10-20LTL

♦ *Kolonada*

Nice restaurant overlooking the Nemunas, has a beautiful patio and sometimes has live music.
Kudirkos g. 22 (this is tucked down the hill near the Europa Royale Hotel)
Main Courses: ~15-30LTL
www.druskininkukolonada.lt

♦ *Keturi Vėjai (Four Winds)*

Restaurant and wine bar situated on the top floor of the Grand Spa Lietuva Hotel – has modern cuisine and a panoramic view of the Druskininkai area.
Main Courses: ~20-35LTL
Kudirkos g. 45 (8th floor of Grand Spa Lietuva)

♦ *Dangaus Skliautas*

Overlooking the Nemunas river with picturesque al fresco dining, a nice wine selection, and some excellent food. It serves a cross between Mediterranean and Lithuanian cuisine.
www.dangaussskliautas.lt
Main Courses: ~15-25LTL

♦ *Forto Dvaras*
One of the chain restaurants that specialize in traditional Lithuanian food, this location has a nice setting overlooking the lake.
Čiurlionio g. 55
Main Courses: ~10-20LTL
www.fortas.eu

♦ *Aero Gallery* (In the Snow Arena)
European cuisine with panoramic view of Druskininkai. Best place to view the vast areas of pine forests that surround Druskininkai.
www.snowarena.lt
Nemuno Kelias 2

Grūtas Park (Stalin World)

This park, commonly known as "Stalin World," is filled with sculptures and other memorabilia from the Soviet era spread over 20 hectares. (Hectares?! A hectare is, of course, 100 ares. You understand now, right?) Grūtas Park is located about 8 km east of Druskinkinkai, just off the A4 in the village of Grūtas. The park was founded by, and is located next to the residence of, the "Mushroom King" of Lithuania, Viliumas Malinauskas.[15] When first opened, the park was somewhat controversial because it was seen by some as glorifying the Soviet past, but Malinauskas expressed his desire to display the statues so that the horrors of the Soviet era would not be forgotten.

---

[15] I don't think he's really called the Mushroom King, but Malinauskas made a lot of money in the years after independence by buying mushrooms from the surrounding areas and exporting them, so I think of him like Abe Froman, the "Sausage King" of Chicago. On a related note, the current mayor of Druskininkai is Malinauskas' son.

Seated Lenin (a rare position for Lenin sculptures), previously located in the center of Druskininkai

The park is an impressive place, but only requires a couple of hours to experience – perhaps a little more if you feel like communing with the random animals in the small zoo. The sculptures of Lenin, Stalin, and various other notable communist figures are arranged along a series of walking paths, and a couple of buildings house interesting posters, pins, busts and other memorabilia. (And, yes, my wife had to wear one of those atrocious and uncomfortable black school uniforms displayed in the museum.) There is also a canteen that serves Soviet-style meals. Admission is 20LTL for adults.

Information is available at www.grutoparkas.lt.

Girios Aidas Forest Museum

This cute little museum, set in a sort of tree house structure, is worth a visit if you have a little extra time on your way to/from

119

Grūto Parkas, Vilnius or Kaunas. The modest museum is packed with taxidermied animals, woodcarvings and other forest things. The museum is located at M. K. Čiurlionio gatvė 116 and is open Tuesday through Sunday. Information is at www.dmu.lt.

Liškiava Church and Monastery

The Church of the Holy Trinity is located about 8km northeast of Druskininkai in Liškiava. The church and the small monastery complex surrounding it are in a picturesque location, set on a hill overlooking the Nemunas river. Not only are the views from the church impressive, but the lavish interior of the small church in a Late Baroque/Rococo style is also quite remarkable. In addition, the vaults contain some interesting religious artifacts.

The monastery complex has guest rooms and a conference center for events. Information about the church and monastery can be found at www.liskiava.lt. The church is open for tours Tuesday through Sunday from 10am until noon and from 2pm to 4pm. Liškiava can be accessed easily by car, and there is also a cruise on the Nemunas that departs from near the Kolonada Restaurant in Druskininkai. The boat departs at 2:30pm everyday except Monday, with a roundtrip duration of about 3 hours, including the time spent at Liškiava. The cruise is run by the tourism company Druskininkų gelmė (+370 612 26982).

Palanga

Sunset at Palanga Pier

Palanga is one of the most popular resorts in Lithuania, drawing many Lithuanians and Russians, as well as a fair amount of
Germans. The town is located on the Baltic coast, and has
some very nice beaches. The main areas of Palanga are rather
hectic, most notably the chaos of Basanavičiaus gatvė. The scene on this pedestrian walkway is one of kids rampaging about
on bikes and pedal carts, carnival games and rides, vendors
hawking sweets and souvenirs, along with countless restaurants,
all to the soundtrack of Russian and Lithuanian pop music.

While you are unlikely to really enjoy Basanavičiaus gatvė unless
you are a Lithuanian teenager or your favorite beer is Tauras (it
is highly unlikely that either of these is the case), it is worth
braving for a few attractions. Basinavičiaus gatvė leads directly
to one of the best-known features of the town: the 470 meter

121

long pier[16] that stretches out into the Baltic. The pier is a beautiful spot from which to watch the sunset. Basanavičiaus gatvė also features a terrific seafood restaurant, Žuvinė, which I recommend. Finally, it's worth stopping by the restaurant Floros Simfonija (it's the one with luxurious landscaping across a small inlet) to get a look at the domesticated rabbits that live on the grassy roofs of some of the buildings. It's very cute.

It is possible to escape the mayhem of Basanavičiaus gatvė and head away from the crowds. There are really nice, flat paths for walking or biking leading along the sea and through pine forests north of Palanga to Šventoji (a much smaller resort town). Access to more secluded beaches is available along the paths. Bike rentals are available throughout the center of the town.

Another opportunity for escaping the crowds is a visit to the Botanical Park and the Amber Museum located in the park. The sprawling park, located just south of the center of town, was founded by Count Feliksas Tiškevičius surrounding his palace. The palace now houses the Amber Museum, which is worth a visit to see the displays of the area's natural resource, even though there are few descriptions in English. Most interesting to me are the displays of inclusions – insects, leaves, and other organic material that were trapped in the sap that became amber. Notice also how the museum seamlessly transitions you from exhibition to gift shop – it's quite deftly conducted.

Information about Palanga can be found at www.palangatic.lt.

---

[16] Amusingly, Lithuanian does not differentiate between a "pier" and a "bridge" (both are **"tiltas"**), so every pier in Lithuania is sort of a bridge to nowhere. While on the subject - there is no tide in the Baltic Sea, so as a result Lithuanian does not really have a word for tide.

Neringa (Nida)

Magnificent dunes of the Curonian Spit

Neringa is perhaps the most strikingly beautiful part of Lithuania. It is well worth a visit if you have the time to make it to this part of the country. The municipality of Neringa incorporates the entire Lithuanian portion of the Curonian Spit (**Kuršių Nerija**) – the narrow, sandy peninsula that stretches for 98 km (61 mi.), 52 km of which is in Lithuania and 46 km of which is in Kaliningrad (Russia). The Spit is separated from the mainland by the Curonian Lagoon (**Kuršių Marios**), a brackish body of water that is fed by the Nemunas River and flows out into the Baltic Sea between Klaipėda and the tip of the Spit. Neringa includes a number of towns and settlements, the most popular and developed of which is Nida, the resort town at the very south of the Lithuanian portion of the Spit. The Curonian Spit is a UNESCO World Heritage Site.

123

The Spit is home to enormous shifting sand dunes – the result of deforestation in the 17th and 18th centuries – that have in the past buried entire villages. Due to reforestation efforts in the 19th century, the dunes have been almost completely tamed and significant portions of the land now have vegetation. The most impressive of the dunes is the Parnidis dune, located just south of Nida. This dune, accessible by foot from Nida along a trail along the water, or by car or bike via Kopų gatvė, reaches a height of 60 meters and provides great views of the sea, lagoon, and the Spit, including the Russian portion of the peninsula. If you look closely, you can see cairns marking the border and occasionally you will see Russians patrolling on ATVs. Don't stray too far without your passport and a visa!

Nida is a beautiful and well-kept resort town, and is significantly more "up-market" than Palanga. During Soviet times, this was one of the resorts reserved primarily for party elites. Whereas people generally go to Palanga to party, visitors go to Nida for a much more relaxed atmosphere. The town is most popular with Lithuanian and German tourists – the area was under German control for centuries prior to 1945. Nida exhibits many old-style wood houses, including the house in which Thomas Mann lived for a couple of summers in the 1930s.

Nida, like the other villages on the Spit, is located on the lagoon side, so there is little in the way of beaches right in town. The beaches on the seaside of the Spit are accessible by car or bike ride – or a tiring walk from Nida (about 2 km (1.25 mi.)). The beaches are organized by levels of clothing (or lack thereof) – look out for the signs as you're walking toward the beach. People swim in the Baltic (although it's usually quite cold!), but not in the lagoon, as that is not considered clean enough for swimming.

Neringa also features nice paths for biking or walking along the forests and dunes. The path from Nida starts in the northern part of town and proceeds through the small villages up the Spit. Along the path near the village of Juodkrantė is the famous Hill of Witches, which is the setting for various fanciful carved wooden sculptures.

Neringa is accessible by ferry from Klaipėda. The drive down the peninsula to Nida can be rather slow and is on a toll road – remember to have some cash with you. A stop in Juodkrantė on the drive to Nida is warranted if you love smoked fish – the town boasts a couple of great shops and restaurants selling the local specialty.

Information about Neringa and Nida is available online at www.visitneringa.com.

Other Areas of Lithuania

There are plenty of other places in Lithuania that are worth visiting, and I regret not being able to write more about these places. In particular, the national parks offer tremendous access to natural areas throughout the country.

I will mention one other place that is quite well-known: the majestic Hill of Crosses (**Kryžių kalnas**) near Šiauliai. This small hill, currently covered with over 100,000 crosses, has for almost two centuries been a site of national and religious significance and is now an important pilgrimage site. Walking among the crosses on the hill is certainly an amazing experience.

Hill of Crosses

Throughout Lithuania, there are natural areas, cities and villages waiting to be explored. I hope you have the opportunity to go out and discover some of the great places off the beaten path. Tell me what I've missed!

Part III

Practical Considerations

Travel Logistics

Citizens of many countries, including the U.S., Canada, Australia, the UK, and other EU countries, do not need visas for tourist visits to Lithuania. Lithuania is part of the Schengen zone, which allows travel throughout the other European countries in Schengen without passport checks at borders. You will likely have your passport checked at your stopover location, and not in Lithuania.

Immediately below in the Flights to Lithuania section, I have provided some advice regarding flights to Lithuania. If you have already secured your means of conveyance to Lithuania, you may want to skip down to Arrival in Vilnius, which provides some useful and money-saving tips.

Flights to Lithuania

Travel to Lithuania from the U.S. and other countries outside of Europe is a bit costly and time consuming. As far as I am aware, there are no regularly scheduled direct flights to Lithuania originating from outside of Europe. This means that your trip will, at a minimum, have one stopover. Because of the long travel time and somewhat severe time zone change, I think it is generally worth paying the premium for a one stopover flight instead of a two stopover flight, though two stopover flights with reasonable layovers can be a decent option.

Fortunately, options for flights to Lithuania from North America are expanding, as more carriers have begun offering flights in recent years. The primary airlines with one stopover flights from the U.S. and Canada to Lithuania are Lufthansa, Finnair,

KLM Royal Dutch, LOT Polish Airlines, SAS, and Aer Lingus. Icelandair has good two stopover flights.

There are also one stopover flights from the U.S. to Lithuania on Aerosvit, a Ukrainian airline, and Aeroflot, a Russian airline, which I mention only to caution you against. The advertised prices are usually the lowest I have seen, but based on the many negative online reviews, these airlines should be avoided. Is it really worth potentially being stranded in an unheated terminal in Kiev to save a few bucks? In addition, visa issues could complicate travel through these countries.

There is currently no Lithuanian airline flying regularly scheduled commercial flights, as they seem to have established a bad habit of going out of business. StarOne Airlines, the most recent attempt at a Lithuanian airline, was abruptly shut down in 2010 when its single plane was impounded by an airport for failing to pay its landing fees. The mayor of Vilnius has recently announced that a new airline, AirLituanica, partly owned by the municipality of Vilnius, is planning to commence operations in the Spring of 2013.

There are, of course, many factors to consider when choosing an airline, including cost, departure and arrival locations, length of itinerary, frequent flyer miles program, in-flight experience, layover locations, number of layovers and total travel time, customer service, and plenty more. Based on my experiences, there is no one airline that is clearly superior in all aspects. On balance, SAS may be the best choice from New York and Washington, DC, and other airlines may be preferable from other locations. Following are descriptions of the airline choices to Lithuania, based on my experiences and the advice of many other travelers with whom I have consulted.

- *In-Flight Experience*: I highly recommend Finnair for its in-flight experience, and KLM and Lufthansa also rate highly. These airlines have the best food and beverage service, and the most comfortable seating. (Be aware though, that some KLM and Lufthansa flights to Europe are operated by U.S. partner airlines – Delta and United, respectively – and those in-flight experiences are not as good as those on actual KLM or Lufthansa flights.) Finnair flies the newest fleet of any European airline – the company claims that its intercontinental fleet is an average of three years old. From my experiences, LOT, Icelandair, and Aer Lingus seem to have the oldest planes, with the SAS planes being slightly newer. The intercontinental flights of Finnair and Lufthansa, and some intercontinental flights of KLM, have seat-back personal entertainment systems with a choice of movies, television shows, games, music, and even a phone. LOT only has the ancient drop down screens every 5 or so rows and on the flights that I have taken with SAS, there were seat-back screens, but they only showed set programming for everyone.

- *Cost*: Airline flight prices obviously vary widely over time and among departure locations, though the relative prices among the airlines tend to be relatively constant. Depending on the location, KLM and Lufthansa are generally in the same price range, with Finnair a little less expensive, then SAS being a bit less expensive, and Icelandair and LOT being least expensive. Strangely, some Aer Lingus flights are relatively quite expensive for the quality of the airline. Prices to Lithuania are generally lowest from New York, a bit higher from cities like Chicago, Boston, and Washington, DC, and ranging higher for other cities.

- *Departure and Arrival Days/Times*: Most airlines have decent departure times from North America and arrival times in Lithuania, so the differentiating factor is the departure times from Lithuania. Finnair has a comfortable departure time of 11:45am from Vilnius, while most other airlines have rough early morning departures from Vilnius, in the 5:30am to 6:30am range. These departure times can be alleviated somewhat by staying in the Vilnius airport hotel the night before departure (see the Departure from Vilnius section below).

- *Airport Transfer*: Finnair is the only airline of which I am aware that usually does not require bus transportation between the plane and the terminal at either the Vilnius airport or the connecting airport, although sometimes a bus is required in Helsinki depending on the gate assigned. This can make a big difference in cold weather and/or precipitation.

- *Stopover Location*: There are a variety of considerations in this category, including how good the airport is, how easy it is to access the stopover city, and options for staying over in the stopover city. I like all of the Scandinavian airports (Helskinki, Copenhagen, and Stockholm) and Amsterdam is very nice as well. Each of these airports also has easy and convenient transportation into the city if you want to visit them. Charles de Gaulle (Paris) should be avoided because it is a terrible hassle. The Warsaw airport is not great. Icelandair often runs package deals that include a couple of days stopover in Iceland in order to promote tourism. As far as I am aware, the Helsinki airport is the only one out of these that has free wireless internet access.

- *Layover Duration and Total Travel Time*: This can be one of the trickiest considerations when choosing an airline and itinerary. There is a definite risk/reward tradeoff. Selecting an itinerary with shorter layover times gives the possibility of a relatively short overall trip time, but also increases the risk that the connecting flight will be missed. It is worth carefully reviewing the layover times and fall-back flights later in the day for the airline you select. There are too many situations to address here, but I will state that for flights from New York, I am much more comfortable with the layover situation with SAS than I am with Finnair. Another aspect to consider is how short each flight leg is, and Icelandair is clearly best in this respect.

- *Customer Service*: I have experienced generally high levels of service on flights to and from Lithuania. Again, Finnair, KLM and Lufthansa generally have the best service. I have also experienced great service from SAS and LOT. I would particularly commend the SAS staff for how they handled our night trapped in the Newark airport during the Snowpocalyse of 2010. The only airline that has stood out to me as having bad customer service is Aer Lingus.

You can, of course, book a flight to Europe and then book a separate flight to Lithuania, which may save you some money, especially if you are planning to also stay for a while in the stopover location. On the other hand, this approach will definitely increase headaches and you will lose the higher baggage allowance that you have on a trans-Atlantic itinerary.[17] Quite a few airlines fly to Vilnius from other European cities. Very inexpensive options if you go this route and don't care about a

---

[17] The free checked baggage allowance for most trans-Atlantic flights is 23kg, and that limit goes down to 20kg or less for most intra-Europe flights. The low cost airlines that fly to Lithuania, such as Aer Lingus, Air Baltic and Ryanair, charge for any checked baggage unless you are booked on these airlines as part of a transatlantic itinerary.

baggage limit are Ryanair, which flies to both Vilnius and Kaunas, and Wizzair, which flies to Vilnius. Be aware, though, that these airlines generally fly from out of the way airports that are not the main airports for a city. Check very carefully whether you would have to change to a different airport if you plan to fly one of these airlines.

One other option, particularly if your destination is in the northern part of the country, would be to fly into Riga, Latvia and take a bus or train to Lithuania. There are many more flight options to Riga than to anywhere in Lithuania.

I recommend www.seatguru.com for reference when selecting seats. This site can help you avoid the dreaded bathroom seats and seats where the entertainment system boxes take up some of your foot space.

Arrival in Vilnius

Upon arrival in Vilnius, you will probably exit through the main gate, Arrival Gate A – if you come though Arrival Gate C, take a right down the hallway to get to Arrival Gate A. Many ATMs and bank kiosks are located here. Baggage storage is located near the elevators. In the left side corner by the doors to the outside is a visitors' information booth, with very handy guides and maps for free. Before you head into town, I would advise having a map in hand.

Most of the rental car companies are located in the hall to Gate C or at Gate C. There are a plethora of taxis stationed outside, ready to take as much money from you as possible. I have heard quotes from them of 60-80LTL (24-32USD) for a trip to the Old Town, which is only about 6km from the airport! My wife and I actually tested them, me asking in English and her asking in Lithuanian, and she got lower quoted rates. If you are able, I would suggest you call or have someone call a taxi to pick you up at the airport. Prices for a called taxi to the Old Town should range between 10-20LTL (4-8USD). Since there is free wireless at the airport (at least in the departure hall, if not also in the arrival hall), you could even Skype call (see Communications) for a taxi if you have a number to call. Taxi services and recommended companies are discussed in the Transportation section.

A great option to the Old Town is the airport shuttle train, which is surprisingly under-advertised but very convenient. (I suspect a conspiracy by the taxi companies to keep the shuttle underutilized.) Last I saw, there is essentially no information about the train in Arrival Gate A, but there was a schedule posted in Arrival Gate C. The station for this new, modern and comfortable train is located a very short walk from the Arrivals Hall, straight ahead on the left side of the road. The train departs approximately every 50 minutes (until about 10pm) and takes passengers to the train station in Vilnius, a short distance from the Old Town. The shuttle costs 2.5LTL and tickets should be purchased on the train. This shuttle is also extremely convenient if your destination is somewhere other than Vilnius, because you can take the shuttle to the train station and connect to another train there.

From the train station, you can walk to the Old Town (especially if you are staying in the southern part of the Old Town) or catch a much less expensive taxi to your ultimate destination. I would caution that the area between the station and the Old Town is a little shadier than the Old Town itself, so although walking during the day should be fine, I would suggest taking a taxi when it is dark.

Departure from Vilnius

The Vilnius airport is a relatively small airport, so moving through the ticketing and security process when departing is usually quick and easy. The airport also has a free scale for your convenience, which can be quite useful for last minute reallocations of weight, in case you are bringing back as much alcohol and chocolate as possible. The scale is located on the right side of the terminal, past the first row of ticket counters and a kiosk, and almost to the security gates. As mentioned above, there is free wireless service in the Vilnius airport, but it does not work so well near some of the peripheral departure gates.

If you have an early morning departure, it is worth considering staying in the airport hotel, Adelita (www.adelita.lt), which is literally a one or two minute walk from the airport. This hotel until recently had a number of old Soviet-era rooms, but it has apparently renovated most rooms as of March 2011. I would advise confirming that you have a renovated room.

The airport maintains a pretty useful website at www.vilnius-airport.lt.

What to Bring

The weather is probably the most important thing to consider when packing for travel to Lithuania. During most of the year, I recommend packing a rain jacket and an umbrella. (Note that Lithuanians don't share the superstition against opening umbrellas inside, so go ahead and give it a try while you're visiting.) If you are visiting in the winter, make sure to pack for very cold weather and slushy unshoveled sidewalks, so a heavy jacket and sturdy boots are likely to be essential.

Lithuania is a modern country, and most small items you might need to buy while traveling are available. However, you may do well to bring most of what you regularly need, because some toiletries, contact lens solution for instance, are relatively expensive.

Some items can be difficult, if not impossible to find. For example, I found that the only way to get a new contact lens case was to buy the expensive lens solution. I advise bringing disposable hand and toe warmers if visiting in the colder months. The toe warmers have been particularly useful. Also, for some reason Lithuanian stores do not seem to sell blank note cards. If you like to use note cards (for making flash cards to study a language, for instance), you will need to import your own.

It may be worth picking up electrical plug adapters before you arrive. Lithuania uses the standard continental European two round prongs plug and 220 volts. Cheap and simple adapters are usually fine, but a converter is necessary for equipment with motors, such as hairdryers. It is usually preferable to use local equipment and avoid dealing with a converter, however, as they are expensive and heavy, and there is still some risk of damage to your equipment.

Money and Buyin' Stuff

The currency of Lithuania is the **litas**, plural **litai**, and is divided into 100 cents (**centai**). Although Lithuania does not use the euro, the litas is pegged at 3.45 litai to the euro, so the value of the litas moves along with the euro. The litas has tended to hover around 1USD/2.5LTL (generally between 2.3 and 2.7 during the last 5 years), which fortunately makes conversion calculations fairly easy.

All prices in Lithuania, as in the rest of Europe, are quoted including sales tax. This makes a lot of sense to me, and makes calculating the actual cost of a purchase so much easier than in the U.S. The receipt will show the amount of Value Added Tax (VAT, or PVM in Lithuanian) that was included in the price. Prices are also presented in the European standard format for numbers, with commas and periods reversed from the North American format – one hundred thousand is 100.000 and one and a half is 1,50.

One thing to consider when making purchases in Lithuania is that the return policies of most stores are far less liberal than those in the U.S. Whereas in the U.S. one can generally assume that something is returnable for a refund unless otherwise noted, in Lithuania it is safest to assume the opposite.

Credit cards are widely accepted, although it is usually limited to Visa and MasterCard. Occasionally, a cashier may be unfamiliar with the type of card you are using and may ask for the PIN code (**PIN kodas**) when a credit card is used. Make sure that your card is swiped instead of stuck into the chip reading part of the machine. In Europe, cards commonly have chips in them and use PIN codes. Apparently, some U.S. credit cards are starting to use chips as well, but it is certainly not widespread. You might have a PIN code for your credit card, but in most cases I suggest just trying to hit whatever button on the keypad is green or has "Enter" or "OK." If this doesn't work, the last four digits of your credit card number might suffice. If that fails, try saying "Ne PIN kodas" to explain that you don't have a PIN code.

Many credit cards charge a 2-3% foreign transaction fee. There are a number of cards out there that do not charge these fees, though, including all Capital One credit cards. Many premium credit cards also do not charge foreign transaction fees.

We have also found a handy way to avoid ATM fees abroad. Many online banks like Ally and ING Direct, as well as those connected with brokerages such as Schwab or Fidelity, charge no fees for withdrawals at ATMs worldwide AND reimburse for the fees charged by the owner of the ATM. I know from experience that Schwab also has very good exchange rates for purchases and ATM withdrawals. These tips should save you a nice bit of change. Of course, read the fine print carefully!

Communications

Cell phone usage is cheap and easy in Lithuania, and internet access is widespread. Virtually any unlocked phone that uses a SIM card can be used in Lithuania with a SIM card that works in Europe.

Inexpensive prepaid packages with a SIM card can be purchased in most stores and kiosks in Lithuania. The options include Labas (www.labas.lt – part of the Bitė network), Ežys (www.ezys.lt – part of the Omnitel network) or Pildyk (www.pildyk.lt – part of the Tele2 network). The Labas website does not have English instructions, whereas the Ežys and Pildyk sites have instructions in English, but only in PDF. We use Pildyk because it also works in other European countries, while the other two options do not. Prepaid accounts can be recharged at the registers in most stores.

Free wireless internet access is available in some coffee shops, including Coffee Inn, and is actually available all over Laisvės alėja, the main pedestrian boulevard in Kaunas. Paid wireless access is also available in many public locations, although payment may be difficult if you do not have a local bank account or cell phone account. If you have a Lithuanian cell phone account (including the prepaid options described above), you can get internet access for 24 hours by paying 5LTL from your phone at designated wireless hotspots operated by a service named Zebra. There is also free wireless internet access in almost all hotels.

I highly recommend using Skype to make international calls via the internet. Calls between Skype accounts are free, and calls from Skype to landlines or cell phones are also easy to make and quite inexpensive. Paid calls on Skype require signing up with Skype and depositing some money into your account, all of which is a painless process.

Calls made to Lithuania from Canada or the U.S. will need to be dialed in the following format: 011-370-XX-XXX-XXX. Calls from Lithuania to the U.S./Canada will be in the format 00-1-XXX-XXX-XXXX.

The format for calls made within Lithuania can be damn confusing. Phone numbers are generally listed as +370 followed by eight digits, consisting of an area code that is one, two, or three digits long, followed by a phone number which is seven, six, or five digits long. As far as I know, Vilnius is the only city with a one-digit area code (5). A couple of cities, including Kaunas (37), have two digit area codes, while most areas have three digit area codes.

If you are calling from a Lithuanian cell phone to any number in Lithuania, you can dial the full number starting with +370 (or you can replace the +370 with the number 8). If calling a landline from another landline within the local area to which you are calling, disregard the +370 and the area code, and only dial the five, six, or seven digit phone number. If you are dialing long distance and/or calling a mobile number from a landline, you will need to replace the +370 with "8" followed by the eight listed digits. For example, "+370 111 55555" would be "55555" locally and "8 111 55555" long distance. To make it even more confusing, the spacing between numbers is not always consistent, so sometimes the example number would be listed as "+370 111 55 555" or "+370 1 115 5555". When in doubt, just try all sorts of combinations and hope that the person who answers speaks English.

Accommodations

I certainly don't claim to be an expert on hotels in Lithuania, since I have not stayed in many during my visits. Nonetheless, I can recommend the Europa Royale group of hotels based on a lot of experience with them.

These four-star hotels are a good value and have quite good service. The Europa Royales in Vilnius and Druskininkai have ideal locations in historic buildings and the Kaunas hotel has a very good location in a modern building: the Vilnius hotel is located between the Gates of Dawn and the Town Hall Square; the Druskininkai hotel is located right off Vilniaus alėja near the Aqua Park; and the Kaunas hotel is near Laisvės alėja and the Akropolis shopping mall. Note that there is no longer a Europa Royale in Klaipėda, even though many maps and guides continue to include it.

In Vilnius, I recommend trying to get a room on the top (fourth) floor, since these rooms have nice balconies with pretty remarkable views of the city. From what I can tell, the hotel does not seem to charge a higher rate for these as compared to rooms on lower floors without these balconies. I would also strongly advise against getting a room on the "first" floor. These rooms are actually on the second floor of the old part of the hotel and, instead of elevator access, require a climb up a narrow winding stairway with unevenly-spaced stairs. The only positive to these rooms is that they do not overlook the street, so are potentially much quieter on a weekend night during the summer when the partying is in full swing.

Information about the Europa Royale hotels is available online at www.groupeuropa.com.

Most hotels in Lithuania provide complimentary wireless internet access and complimentary breakfasts.

I recommend www.hotels.com or www.tripadvisor.com for hotel searches.

Transportation

Lithuania has a developed system of transportation, but it is not as easily comprehensible by a visitor as it is in most Western European countries.

For traveling between major cities, trains are actually quite good and reasonably priced. The main rail lines include Vilnius, Kaunas, Šiauliai, and Klaipėda, with stops in many of the towns along the way. Smaller rail lines cover other cities, such as Panevėžys, Marijampolė, Šilutė, Rokiškis, and Mažeikiai. A full route map can be accessed on www.litrail.lt, though it is a little tricky to find. You will need to go to the "Route search," search for any route, then click on the "Route map" above the results.

Note that you should take the newer and faster trains (**greitasis traukinys**), and not the diesel trains, which are older and slower. Unfortunately, it is not clear online which is which, so you may need to purchase tickets at the station to be sure. Note also that trains get packed full of students on Friday and Sunday nights, so you may need to purchase tickets in advance for travel during these times. Tickets can be purchased online or in the stations, or on the trains for a slightly higher price. Information on timetables and prices can be accessed at www.litrail.lt.

Options for travel to towns that do not have rail service are buses or taxis. Travel by bus is relatively inexpensive, but takes some effort on the part of a foreigner to figure out. There are a number of buses that will whisk you off to Palanga if you are looking to go to the seacoast and buses to Druskininkai are also readily available. Information about buses to and from Vilnius can be found at www.autobusustotis.lt/en.

Within the major cities, walking will generally be your best option. Biking is possible in some places, as there are well-marked bike lanes in parts of the cities, but Lithuania is certainly not as bike-friendly as some countries, such as the Netherlands. Taxis are your best option for traveling a bit farther. As described above, the shuttle train from the Vilnius airport is a great option that should not be overlooked.

In Lithuania, taxis are rarely hailed on the street – they are usually called for pick-ups. Ask a local friend or your hotel to call for taxi service if you'd rather not try it yourself. Hotels often have arrangements with taxi companies, so you will probably get a trustworthy company at a decent price, but not the cheapest possible. Another trick is to find a line of waiting taxis and just call the numbers posted on the cars, as this will circumvent the higher fees for picking up the taxi on the street.

Prices do vary and may be higher for foreigners. In Vilnius, a reasonable charge for a called taxi is around 1.8LTL/km, though there are indications that the standard prices will be going up in the near future to at least 2LTL/km. The price for a standing taxi can be 3-5 times higher. Note that taxi companies have multiple phone numbers corresponding to each mobile phone company and the landline phone company. Any of the numbers can be used, but if you call from a mobile phone, it is cheaper to call the number for the mobile provider you use. The phone numbers provided below are general numbers; numbers for specific mobile carriers can be found on the websites.

Recommended taxi companies in Vilnius are:

♦ *Taksi Ekipažas* (+370 52 395 539) – www.ekipazastaksi.lt – Cheap and reliable, but with older cars (almost invariably a mid- to late-90s Audi, but you may get to ride in a "Wolksvagen" (see the website)).

♦ *Standart Taksi* (+370 52 400 004) – Slightly more expensive than Taksi Ekipažas, but with newer cars.

Recommended taxi companies in Kaunas are:

♦ *Romo Taksi* (+370 65 644 333) – Older cars, but reliable.

♦ *Euro Taksi* (+370 37 311 111) – www.eurotaksi.lt

♦ *Taksi Kelyje* (+370 37 366 666) – http://taksikelyje.lt – The website has a useful system for making reservations and estimating prices.

♦ *Žaibiškas Greitis* (+370 37 333 111) – www.zaibiskasgreitis.lt

There are no subway systems in Lithuania, but there are buses and **mikriukai** (semi-private minibuses) that run within the cities, both of which would be adventurous choices for someone who does not speak Lithuanian. Should you be interested in riding a bus or minibus in Vilnius, plenty of information about routes and prices is available at www.vilniustransport.lt. Tickets for buses can be purchased at most kiosks or on the bus for a slightly higher price. If you do ride a bus, or hang out long enough at a bus stop (okay, that sounds weird), you might witness an interesting scene: occasionally, transit police will conduct a ticket check on the buses. This usually entails burly female officers blocking the bus doors to prevent the escape of ticketless riders. Anyone found without a ticket is yanked off the bus and put into a parked police van to be fined.

Mikriukai are private vans that drive set numbered routes throughout the cities for a flat rate. They began in early post-Soviet times as a quicker and more comfortable alternative to buses, essentially mimicking the bus routes. More recently, municipal governments are more strictly regulating mikriukai, leading to more standardization and consolidation of the provider companies.

Driving

Driving in Lithuania is a bit chaotic, but not to the extreme of some other countries in Eastern Europe. The average Lithuanian driver is fairly aggressive and less risk averse than the average American driver. When driving in Lithuania, I tend to feel like I am always on the edge of calamity – I just try to reach a state of Zen acceptance that I'll be in an accident at some point. Traffic fatalities in Lithuania are among the highest in the world.

There is likely a cultural explanation for part of the risk taking, but I think another significant factor is probably related to the condition of the roads in Lithuania. It is evident that the road system in Lithuania was not designed for either the volume or speed of traffic that exists today. Most problematically, a majority of the roads are two lane roads that do not have areas widened to include a passing lane. This fact, coupled with the heavy volume of mixed traffic (cars driving significantly over the speed limit, new drivers, truckers legally limited to lower speeds, local and long distance traffic, and the occasional horse-drawn cart) seems to lead to a great deal of passing, often with oncoming traffic not far off. Occasionally Lithuanians adopt the phenomenon I found to be widespread in Estonia: drivers passing on a two lane road create a *de facto* third lane in the center, expecting both the car being passed and oncoming traffic to yield to the sides of the roadway. It can be quite a harrowing experience if you're not expecting it!

There are only two highways with extended sections that would be considered "limited access" (that is, with access limited by well-designed on- and off-ramps), on which true highway speeds are appropriate (on the A1 between Kaunas and Klaipėda and on the A2 between Vilnius and Panevėžys). Some other highways, such as the one between Vilnius and Kaunas, are divided highways but not limited access.

In many parts of the cities, parking also seems quite chaotic. As with the road system, the parking infrastructure in Lithuania was not designed for the volume of vehicles that exists today. Some sidewalks officially serve a dual purpose, with parking spaces painted diagonally right on them. Cars routinely park with the front 2/3 of the car on the sidewalk and the back 1/3 on the street. In other areas, it is quite common to see cars parallel parked straddling the curb. If it appears that other cars are making their own parking spaces, I generally assume it's fine for me to do so as well.

Where there actually are real parking spaces, for some reason Lithuanians almost always back into them. I've never gotten a straight answer as to why this is the case. I suppose this makes for a much quicker departure, but it certainly seems a bit complicated overall.

As in other European countries, gasoline (**benzinas**) prices are higher than in the U.S. – at least 50% more expensive than gasoline in the U.S. Also like other countries, diesel fuel (**dyzelinas**) is much more commonly used in passenger vehicles than in the U.S. and is actually less expensive than gasoline. Fuel stations are generally very modern, and one nice feature rarely found in the U.S. is that almost all provide disposable plastic gloves for pumping the fuel. This is good because a recent study found that gas pump handles are the germiest things that most Americans handle on a regular basis.

You might notice that the octane ratings for gasoline in Lithuania appear to be substantially higher than those in North America. Fuel is of a higher octane, but not by as much as it might seem, because the ratings used in Lithuania represent a different measurement. An octane rating in Lithuania is equal to an octane rating of 4-5 less in North America.[18] The minimum octane available in Lithuania is 95 (equivalent to 90-91 in North America.).

---

[18] In the U.S., the octane rating published is the average of the Research Octane Number (RON) and the Motor Octane Number (MON), usually expressed (R+M)/2. In Lithuania, and most of Europe, the RON is published. The MON for a specific fuel is generally 8-10 less than the RON for the same fuel, therefore an 89 in the U.S. is equivalent to 93 or 94 in Lithuania.

One other fact regarding fuel to note: fuel efficiency is expressed in Lithuania as liters/100km, not miles per gallon, so a bit of converting is required to make sense of how much fuel your vehicle is consuming. For example, 6L/100km is approximately 39 mpg, and it is not uncommon to achieve such high fuel efficiency.

Tourist visitors to Lithuania are permitted to drive with their foreign driver's licenses. Visitors staying for longer may need additional documentation.

Traffic laws and signs are generally understandable and common sense. A few rules/signs/tips to highlight for foreigners:

- On most roads, the speed limit is 50km/h in towns and 90km/h outside of towns. These numbers are rarely posted, but a white rectangular sign with black lettering indicates that you are entering a town. A similar sign with a diagonal line through it indicates that you are leaving the town. Blue signs with the name of a town indicate that you are entering a town, but that no reduction in speed is required.

- The speed limit on the major highways (indicated by a green sign showing a highway with a bridge over it that looks like an "H") is 110km/h. During the summer, the speed limit on the limited access Kaunas-Klaipėda and Vilnius-Panevėžys highways is 130km/h – an exhilarating 80mph.

- Headlights are required at all times.

- Turning right at a red light is not allowed unless there is a small white sign with a green arrow pointing right.

- Lithuanian traffic lights have a very handy feature not found in many other countries: when a light is changing from red to green, it has a short intermediate step when both red and yellow are lit for a second or two. This is pretty useful, especially when driving a car with a manual transmission (which most cars are in Lithuania), as it gives a little extra time to get into gear. Be aware that Lithuanians generally treat the red-yellow combination the same as a green and just start driving.

- It is customary for cars to flash their headlights to warn other drivers of police checking speeds. I'm sure this reflects a tradition of fighting against the authority of the state, but it is probably also common because police running radar are so easy to see. By law, they are not allowed to hide while looking for speeders. In fact, they have an odd setup of one officer in the parked car running radar, while another officer stands by the side of the road with a little stop sign paddle in his hand ready to direct you to pull over.

- Strangely, although police are not allowed to hide to catch speeders, there are a number of mounted radar guns with cameras on the roads, mostly on the highways around Kaunas and Vilnius. On the other hand, these radar guns are all marked with signs warning you about them about 150-200 meters before them. The signs, logically, look like radar waves hitting a car or motorcycle.

- Watch out for moose, especially when driving at highway speeds. I had a very close call with one of the leggy bastards late one night.

- Snow tires are mandatory during the winter, which makes sense, because snow removal from the roads is pretty lackluster. Lithuanians seem pretty adept at just nonchalantly sliding their cars around city streets, occasionally bumping into one another. I have to assume that snow tires are also required for planes, because the Vilnius airport doesn't seem to plow its runways either.

- Drinking and driving is a huge no-no in Lithuania. The BAC limit is 0.04%, and Lithuanians are quite cautious about having anything to drink before driving. Amazingly, for a culture that condones drinking as much as Lithuanians do, this rule is taken very seriously. Breathalyzers are sold at kiosks in many shopping malls.

Dining Out

I tend to go for restaurants that serve traditional Lithuanian food, since it's rare to have an opportunity to have it outside the country, but there are plenty of fine restaurants that serve international cuisine, especially in Vilnius. In the sections above for Vilnius, Kaunas, and Druskininkai, I have included many restaurant recommendations of mine and of Lithuanian friends and family members. Below is some general commentary and advice regarding dining out in Lithuania.

Restaurants of all types in Lithuania provide a very good value. A substantial dinner with a beer at a decent restaurant can often be had for 20-30LTL (~8-12 USD). Remember, of course, that tax is included in all prices listed on the menu.

Most cafés (**kavinė(s)**) have relaxed atmospheres, allowing patrons to leisurely enjoy anything from a beer or coffee to beer snacks to a full meal. In practice, there is often little difference between a kavinė and a casual **restoranas** (restaurant), though a higher end restaurant will clearly show itself to be in a different class.

Somewhat surprisingly, traditional Lithuanian cuisine remains popular, with many chain and local restaurants serving up all the cepelinai, balandėliai, kepta duona, etc. that you could want. Chains focusing on traditional food include Čili Kaimas, Forto Dvaras and Bernelių Užeiga, each of which provides good food at reasonable prices, though it is certainly not the best that you can get in Lithuania. Many local options for traditional fare, such as the more expensive (and far better) Žemaičiai (on Vokiečių gatvė in Vilnius) and less expensive Pilies Menė (on Pilies gatvė in Vilnius), compete favorably with the chains.

I often enjoy ordering what are considered "snacks" on the menu. These often can be ordered as platters, including "beer snacks," which usually include kepta duona, some sort of dried meat, pigs ears, smoked cheese, and some other things; "vodka snacks," which usually include pickles (**rauginti agurkai**), some sort of dark bread, maybe herring and other stuff; or "wine snacks," which often have cheese, cured meat, crackers and other snacks. Unlike on menus in many other countries, these foods that would be considered "appetizers" are usually found toward the back of menus, with the drinks list.

Pizza restaurants have taken off in Lithuania, or, as Lithuanians might say, they have "mushroomed." Most of the chain restaurants are rather similar, though they have some marginal differentiations. In actuality, "pizza" restaurants are generally just regular restaurants that serve a wide variety of food, including many traditional Lithuanian dishes, in addition to pizza. Čili Pica, CanCan Pizza, Mambo Pizza and Charlie Pizza are each a good mainstream choice with low prices, while Pizza Jazz is a bit more upscale.

Tipping is now considered by most to be standard practice, but it is still a custom in transition. As opposed to the 15-20% often left in North America, something more like 5-10% is the norm in Lithuania, with even just a litas or two being perfectly acceptable. What has been stressed to me is that tipping is not really thought of in terms of percentages by Lithuanians. In practice, this seems to mean that tips as a percentage of the bill are usually higher at the low end (for example 1LTL on a 10LTL bill or 2 LTL on 20LTL bill), but that the percentage will be lower on higher bills (for example 5 or 6 LTL on 100LTL bill). Although 10% or more is on the high end, if I receive a bill for only, say, 30LTL (~12 USD) and have had a good meal, leaving 3LTL (just over 1 USD) feels to me like a small addition to the price. Note that no matter what, you should never leave "white change" (1, 2 and 5 cent pieces), as that is considered insulting. Occasionally at high-end restaurants a service charge will be added to the bill, in which case no additional tip should be given.

For your tips, you will generally have been provided prompt, though somewhat aloof, service. I have observed, though, that service in restaurants seems to have improved noticeably within the last few years, and certainly exceeds the standard of service in much of Southern Europe. (Perhaps there's some correlation with an increase in tipping?) In most casual restaurants and cafés, you should seat yourself at whichever table you prefer with no need to wait for the staff to seat you. Surprisingly, wait staff are quite attuned to the arrival of customers, and you will quickly be given a menu and perhaps asked if you would like something to drink. If you are asked this in Lithuanian, I suggest you simply say "**Švyturio Ekstra didelis, prašom**". You will be off to a delicious and refreshing start to the meal and will have simultaneously signaled that you are not Lithuanian, owing to your butchering of the pronunciation and grammar. (Should you want to be more subtle, you can simply place a guidebook printed in English on the table; should you want to be less subtle, you can wear a cowboy hat emblazoned with the American flag.)

Almost all wait staff you encounter will speak English, but will be happy to humor your attempts at pronouncing the dishes. During your meal, do not expect a cheerful "How is everything?" accompanied by an ingratiating smile from your server. It will generally be your responsibility to flag your server down if you need something, but an empty glass on your table will usually bring him or her around in short order. You can ask for the check by saying "**Sąskaitą, prašom**" ("Check, please").

If you are paying with a credit card, the server will bring a remote card reading machine to the table instead of taking your card away. This is a fairly common practice in Europe. The transaction will probably go smoothly, but occasionally servers try to process your card like a card with a chip in it, so you may have to remind them to swipe it instead.

One aspect of restaurants with outdoor seating that seems to be quite unique to Lithuania and other Northern European countries is the availability of blankets. Essentially every restaurant with outdoor seating has plenty of soft, cozy blankets available for use. Most restaurants also have heat lamps for outdoor seating.

A few minor, but potentially aggravating, differences between U.S. and Lithuanian restaurants should be noted and accepted before you sit down to eat in Lithuania. Water is generally not complimentary in Lithuanian restaurants (as it is not in much of Europe). If you would like water, you will probably need to order mineral water in your choice of carbonated (**gazuotas**) or still (**negazuotas**). It is, however, becoming more common for people to ask for tap water, so you could try requesting that if you like. There may be a charge for it or it might be complimentary. Water is rarely served with ice, but if you are wearing the aforementioned cowboy hat, your server may very well know you want ice. Also, there are generally no free refills for whatever beverage you ordered. Finally, there usually is no option for "doggy bags," although this may be available for pizza. Regarding the water issue, I have come to accept this as a function of paying for what you want and not bundling the price of serving water in with the meals. However, it is still a bit of a shock to find that a nice draft beer costs the same as, or less than, bottled water in a restaurant. As for the lack of doggy bags, it appears to be a bit of a cultural carry-over, coupled with the fact that portions are rarely as gargantuan as those in the U.S.

Grocery Shopping

You can find the locations of the specific food shopping locations mentioned below on the Vilnius Places of Interest map available at www.experiencinglithuania.com.

I highly advise a trip to a Lithuanian grocery store – it's a great way to get acquainted with some of the interesting food available in the country. Forget whatever image you may have in your mind about Soviet-style food stores. Stores in Lithuania are incredibly modern, and could be mistaken for any store in Western Europe.

Prominent grocery store chains include Maxima, Iki, and to a lesser extent, Rimi. Maxima and Iki stores come in fairly well-specified sizes: Maximas are designated X, XX, or XXX for sizes from small (like a convenience store) to large, and Ikis are designated "Ikiukas" for small, and simply "Iki" for larger stores.[19] Some of these chains even have super-sized "Hyper" versions of these stores. The larger versions of these stores often have a number of small, specialized shops in the same building around their perimeters.

If you are interested in visiting a grocery store while in the Old Town of Vilnius, I recommend going to the Maxima XXX located on Mindaugo gatvė between Jono Basanavičiaus gatvė and Naugarduko gatvė. There is also a small Rimi very centrally located in the Old Town at the Town Hall Square.

Another great place to shop for food is the Tymo (Užupis) Eco Farmers' Market, located at the intersection of Aukštaičių gatvė and Maironio gatvė in Užupis. Here you can find fresh, high-quality fruits, vegetables, breads, cheeses, smoked meats, and many other products. The market operates on Thursdays from 12-6pm all year round. If you're feeling adventuresome, there is a large market (**Halės Turgus**) on the corner of Pylimo g. and Bazilijonų g. that is open most days and features vendors selling a wide variety of foods, drinks and other goods.

Beer, wine and liquor are all available for sale in grocery stores, but it should be noted that, although sales of alcohol are permitted on every day of the week, <u>alcohol cannot be purchased</u>

---

[19] A couple of random facts: 1) the Maxima stores used to be Minima, Media, and Maxima, but were standardized, and 2) "Iki" means "see you later," (literally "until") and thus "Ikiukas" means "little see you later."

in stores after 10pm. Bars and restaurants are, of course, permitted to sell alcohol after that time.

You will likely notice that food produced in Lithuania is quite
inexpensive. While you wander the store, look out for the following snacks/sweets that I fancy (these are my idiosyncratic
personal favorites, your tastes may vary):

- *Dadu* ice cream (**ledai**) – These are inexpensive ice cream
  treats in strange little cones, and are throwbacks to the type
  of ice cream treats commonly available during Soviet times.
  The ice cream is quite light and airy. I recommend the original vanilla (labeled "plombyras"). These will be found in
  coolers near the registers or in the frozen section, and are also often available from street vendors.

- Varškės treats (**sūreliai** – literally "little cheeses") – These are
  cold, sweet treats covered in chocolate based on **varškė**,
  which is a type of light, mild cheese that is generally not
  available in the U.S., though it is similar to what is sold as
  "farmer's cheese." There is a very wide variety of these – I
  recommend ones with poppy seeds, but there are plenty of
  tasty choices. These will be found in the refrigerated dairy
  section.

- Pastries/buns (**bandelės**) – There are lots of great baked
  goods available at most grocery stores. Some of the best local
  pastries include **šokoladinės bandelės** (chocolate buns) and
  bandelės su aguonomis (buns with poppy seeds). Many
  pastries incorporate poppy seeds in some way.

- Rye Bread (**ruginė duona**) – Lithuanian rye bread is quite
  different from the typical rye bread found in American su-

permarkets. This very dark, dense bread plays a central role in Lithuanian cuisine, and is consumed much more often than light wheat breads. There are a myriad of variations of this bread available at any grocery store. Rye bread baked on a layer of calamus leaves (**ajerų duona**) is considered a specialty for festive occasions.

- *Javinukai* – These pre-packaged treats don't really have an analogue in the U.S. – they don't really fit into a category of snacks. *Javinukai* are long pillows of baked flour with different sweet flavorings injected into the center. My favorite flavors are chocolate and milk (**pieniniai**). These are usually found near the packaged breads.

- Cocoa shells cereal (**kakavinės kriauklelės** or **kakaviniai javainiai**) – These are pretty straightforward – a tasty, mildly sweet cocoa cereal that is common throughout Europe but not found in the U.S. Yes, they are clearly marketed to children, as evidenced by the cartoon mice and other critters on the packaging.

In general, food in Lithuania and Europe is more natural than food in North America, probably based both on consumer choice and regulations. It is likely not a coincidence that fruits and vegetables generally taste much better than in North America. You may notice that a lot of products have claims such as "Be konservantų," "Ekologiška," or "Be E". These mean "Without preservatives," "Organic" and "Without additives". Foods also must disclose whether they contain genetically modified ingredients.

The "E" system in Europe is quite interesting. Each additive (color, preservative, emulsifier, flavor enhancer, etc.) approved for food use in the EU is assigned an E number. Foods without E are the most natural. Note that an additive is not necessarily a bad thing, but it does signify that there is something added from the product's (or its component parts') natural ingredients. For instance, turmeric and Vitamin C are likely harmless, and potentially beneficial, but both are E if they are added to the food product.

Note also that "E" should not be confused with the large "e" that is often included near the weight or volume on a product's packaging. This "e" or "e-mark" stands for "estimated," and signifies that the contents of the package contain approximately the amount indicated, within an accepted range, in accordance with an EU regulation. (And with just these two examples, you can see how heavily food is regulated in the EU.)

When you get to the checkout, there are a few things to keep in mind. First, you will need to purchase grocery bags if you want them. Usually, a couple sizes will be hanging by or below the register for you to select. Just put them with the stuff you are buying and they will be scanned. Second, very few cashiers at grocery stores speak English. That's fine. They may ask you a question if they don't realize that you aren't Lithuanian – it will probably be whether you have a rewards card for the store. I assume you do not, so just shake your head, smile like a fool, and hand them money or swipe your card. After this, you will have to bag your own groceries.

I had one rather ridiculous incident at the checkout in a Maxima where my Lithuanian language skills were stretched to their limit. I went in to purchase a phone credit for my wife to add to her pre-paid phone account. As I was feeling pretty confident in my ability to navigate the buying process in Lithuania, my wife stayed in our apartment and sent me a text message with the instructions of what to tell the cashier. When I got in line, I wasn't purchasing any items, so I just stood in line with my phone practicing what I needed to say. When it got to be my turn, the cashier looked at me, and assuming the items on the belt were mine, she started scanning the items for the person behind me. I shook my head and said "neh, neh," but stepped aside for the person behind me to check out. After she completed that order, the cashier glared at me once more and again reached for items of the next person behind me, beginning with a pair of white lacy panties! Unfortunately, I hadn't yet learned "Those are not my white lacy panties" in Lithuanian, so I was restricted to more frantic "Neh! Neh!" in order to stop her. In the end I was able to struggle through relaying my request and make the purchase. After a nod to the customer behind me with the unusual grocery store purchase, I was on my way.

Time

Lithuania is in the Eastern European time zone, which is 7 hours ahead of the U.S. East Coast for most of the year. For short periods surrounding the changeovers from and to daylight savings time, Lithuania is only 6 hours ahead of the East Coast. Lithuania switches to daylight savings time approximately two weeks later than the U.S. in the spring and switches from DST approximately one week earlier than the U.S. in the autumn.

Europeans generally use the 24-hour clock, which after some adjustment will make perfect sense to the newcomer. Although it seemed odd to me at first coming from a 12-hour system, I came to realize the efficacy of using a system that leaves less

159

room for confusion (apparently the U.S. military figured this out long ago). However, despite the use of the 24-hour clock in writing, Lithuanians do refer to time in speech according to the 12 hour system. Thus, in colloquial speech, 19:00 would be referred to as 7 in the evening and not as 19 o'clock.

Dates in Lithuania are written Year/Month/Day or Day/Month/Year, as in 2012/05/20 or 20/05/12 (May 20, 2012).

In contrast to the U.S. (and English language-centric) system of referring to the days of the week in short form as M, T, W, etc., Lithuanian retail establishments refer to the days of the week with the Roman numerals I-VII, with Monday being I and Sunday being VII. Of course, this system benefits the non-Lithuanian speaker greatly, as you would likely have a hard time deciphering P, A, T, etc. (pirmadienis, antradienis, trečiadienis, etc.)![20] In addition, instead of using Roman numerals, businesses will sometimes simply post their opening days as seven symbols in a row or column, often showing a half day in the sixth symbol (Saturday) and no opening in the seventh symbol (Sunday).

One other interesting fact about Lithuanian timekeeping is that the seasons "officially" start on March 1, June 1, September 1, and December 1. In the U.S., on the other hand, our "official" seasons begin and end with solstices and equinoxes. Although I am used to the U.S. system, it's not entirely clear to me why the summer should officially start in the U.S. on the day which most of Northern Europe refers to as "Midsummer."

---

20 The days of the week Monday through Sunday are: pirmadienis, antradienis, trečiadienis, ketvirtadienis, penktadienis, šeštadienis, sekmadienis – literally "first day" through "seventh day."

Safety

I am including a section on safety not because you really need to be concerned about crime (just be sensible as you would elsewhere), but because it's worth being aware that you are more responsible for your own safety in Lithuania than you are in North America, especially in the U.S. By this, I mean that as a result of being a less litigious society, you are not protected as much from obvious dangers as you are in the U.S.

In general, if there is a common-sense danger, there will not be a big sign warning you of it. Practically anywhere I look in Lithuania, I see something that would be covered, or locked, or have a big warning stuck on it, or not exist at all in the U.S. For instance, you won't see a big sign by a cliff that reads "DAN-GER – CLIFF" and there probably won't be a fence by it. I've seen big heating elements in saunas with very little protection against falling on them. Heavy-duty fireworks are easy to acquire at party stores. Champagne bottles don't tell you that you shouldn't point them at your face when opening them. Coffee cups don't warn you that coffee is hot. You get the picture. Don't forget to look both ways when crossing the street...

Also, as I have already mentioned, you can generally swim wherever you want. There usually won't be lifeguards, nor will there be signs telling you that you are swimming at your own risk, nor will someone require you to sign a waiver. A few places to which I have directed you do sometimes have lifeguards, including the Green Lakes and Vijūnėlės pond in Druskinkinai, but those lifeguards are unlikely to be constantly blowing their whistles or harassing people to stop their "horseplay" or other such nonsense common in the U.S. If a lifeguard does yell at you, I suggest you just yell back "Aš nesuprantu lietuviškai!" and go back to whatever you were doing.

One other safety issue in Lithuania that has caught my attention is the drastically different fire safety standards, specifically for restaurants and bars located in old cellars. These are beautiful locations for dining or drinking, but unfortunately they generally have only one exit, making the possibility of an emergency departure quite difficult. This concern is exacerbated if you happen to find yourself in a certain lounge in the Vilnius Old Town that seems to specialize in flaming drinks.

If you do happen to need assistance, perhaps due to accidentally falling off a cliff, dial 112 for emergency services. If you need an ambulance, you can ask for a **greitoji pagalba** (literally "fast help").

Entertainment

Lithuania has a variety of entertainment options, generally comparable with other European countries. The most sophisticated live performances are mostly found in Vilnius.

Large, modern movie theaters are available throughout Lithuania – mostly located in shopping malls in or near the major cities. Most movies are in English with Lithuanian subtitles, and the release dates for movies are not far behind those in the U.S. One twist in Lithuanian movie theaters is that tickets are usually purchased for specific seats. Therefore, it can be a good idea to purchase your tickets a bit in advance to get a better seat. I don't think there is any differential in prices among seat locations.

Three Muses in front of the National Drama Theatre

Lithuania does have some fairly good theater companies and orchestras, although I have not been to enough shows to provide much commentary. In Vilnius, the main venue for larger theater productions is the Lithuanian National Drama Theatre (**Lietuvos nacionalinis dramos teatras**) on Gedimino prospektas. The website for the theater is at www.teatras.lt, but unfortunately no English is available so you'll have to try navigating in Lithuanian. Also in Vilnius, the country's primary venue for orchestral performances is the National Philharmonic Hall (**Nacionalinė filharmonija**), located on Aušros Vartų gatvė (www.filharmonija.lt). Prominent ballets and operas are staged at the Lithuanian National Opera and Ballet Theatre (**Lietuvos nacionalinis operos ir baleto teatras**), located on A. Vienuolio gatvė (just off Gedimino prospektas) (www.opera.lt). Outside of these large venues, there are plenty of smaller venues throughout the country that host concerts and theatrical performances.

Non-classical music (rock, pop, etc.) is often performed in clubs or at larger venues like sports stadiums. Smaller venues in Vilnius include Tamsta Klubas (www.tamstaclub.lt), which closes in the summer for some reason, Brodvėjus, and St. Catherine's church (Šv. Kotrynos bažnyčia). Large song festivals are held in amphitheaters in parks on the outskirts of Vilnius. Good schedules of events in Vilnius and throughout the country can be found at www.bilietai.lt/en/, www.bilietupasaulis.lt, and www.vilnius-events.lt.

For those so inclined, another possible form of entertainment is casinos, which have popped up all over the major cities in Lithuania. You will likely need your passport to be able to register to play.

If you are interested in getting a taste of the music currently popular in Lithuania, there are a few prominent radio stations available. M-1 (www.m1.lt) and Radiocentras (www.rc.lt) play a mix of popular American, European and Lithuanian music. M-1 Plius (www.pliusas.fm) is aimed at an older crowd, and plays mostly new and past rock hits (primarily American). Both of the M-1 sites provide online streaming of the station's programming and also have a list of the station frequencies throughout Lithuania.

Lithuania has produced some very good musical artists in recent years. Popular performers include Andrius Mamontovas, Marijonas Mikutavičius, Mantas Jankavičius, Lemon Joy, Rasabasa, KeyMono (formerly BrassBastardz), Jurga, G&G Sindikatas, The Ball & Chain, Sel, Leon Somov & Jazzu, and Skylė (often performing with Aistė Smilgevičiūtė). Two of my favorites are Andrius Mamontovas and Jurga. Mamontovas has been performing since well before independence as a member of the

164

legendary band Foje, and is now a well-established and popular rock musician, as well as an actor and producer. Jurga Šeduikytė, known simply as Jurga, is a singer/songwriter who came to prominence in the early 2000s and had her first album produced by Mamontovas in 2005. I also really like RasaBasa and KeyMono.

Most of these performers sing at least some of their songs in English and there is a lot of collaboration with non-Lithuanian artists. An interesting aspect of Lithuanian music is that there is a fair amount of patriotism and passion for Lithuania that is exhibited. For example, Marijonas Mikutavičius has a popular song titled "Aš Tikrai Myliu Lietuva" ("I Really Love Lithuania"). This is certainly much less common in American music, at least outside of country music. I think the relatively small size and recent independence of Lithuania encourage Lithuanian singers to sing about the country in this way.

Bathroom Matters

If you are like most people, you will likely visit a bathroom at least a few times while in Lithuania, so it's worth preparing you for some of their idiosyncrasies. I think the Lithuanian bathroom has to be a practical joke – it is simply too full of pitfalls and inefficiencies to not be. Many of the traits I describe below are actually common throughout Europe, but may seem odd to a North American.

- *Shower curtains* – For some reason, Lithuanians, and many Europeans in general, don't use shower curtains in their showers. This is one thing I just don't get and I'll go ahead and assert that they are wrong about it. I'm curious as to how Lithuanians take showers without splashing everywhere –

165

perhaps they just stand stiff like a board and hope the water finds its way where it should. ("In Soviet Lithuania, you don't take shower, shower take you!") I do recognize that Europeans have a fondness for baths, as opposed to showers, but it certainly seems like they could recognize that many people have moved beyond 19th century bathing habits. If you are staying in a hotel, I encourage you to do your part in convincing the Lithuanians of their folly by splashing about in your shower like a frisky mer-person. Perhaps if they have to deal with water all over the bathrooms they will finally come to their senses.

- *Toilets* – You might notice that toilets in Lithuania tend to be the low-flow variety. As in most of Europe, toilets actually have two buttons with options for ultra-low-flow or just simply very-low-flow. This can take some getting used to if, like many Americans, you are accustomed to using hundreds of gallons of water each flush. While this is good for water conservation and cost savings, it isn't quite as effective as our profligate American approach. You will often need to clean up a bit with the toilet brush, which is conveniently provided next to essentially every toilet (even in public bathrooms).

- *Light switches* – Essentially all bathrooms in Lithuania have the light switches outside of the bathroom. What purpose can this possibly serve? I know some bathrooms have this in North America as well, but it's weird here too.

- *Closed doors* – Even in private homes, Lithuanians often fully close the bathroom door when no one is inside. Perhaps that's why light switches are all on the outside – so you can tell by the switch if someone is in the bathroom?

- *Slippery bathtubs* – Bathtubs in Lithuania rarely have the no-slip surfaces that are common in North America. Again, this is probably related to Lithuanians' affinity for baths.

- *Toilet paper* – Lithuanians seem to quite often opt for some relatively, shall we say, harsh toilet paper. My father speculates that the country must be still working its way through a massive stockpile of Soviet-era TP.

The one advantage that Lithuanian bathrooms may have over North American bathrooms is that a fair number of them have heated floors and heated towel racks. This is really nice on cold days, especially if you've slipped in the shower and you're lying incapacitated on that nice heated floor.

Bookstores and Guides

Bookstores in Lithuania provide a great opportunity to pick up guides and other books about Lithuania in English at generally reasonable prices. I've found the Pegasas chain of bookstores to generally have the best selection of English language books, though some of the Vaga stores also have a fairly wide selection.

In Kaunas, Vilnius, and Klaipėda, there are smaller Pegasas shops located in the old towns (and on Laisvės alėja in Kaunas), but the largest shops with the best selection are in the Akropolis malls. There are also Pegasas shops in many other towns throughout the country. Vaga has shops throughout Vilnius, including on Gedimino prospektas, Pilies gatvė, and in the Europa, Gedimino 9, and Ozas malls. There also happens to be a small bookshop in the departure terminal of the Vilnius airport (inside security), which for some reason has books in English that I have not found elsewhere.

There are some good conventional guides to Lithuania available, though I am still eagerly waiting for Rick Steves to enter the fray. The best may be the Bradt guide *Lithuania*, by Gordon McLachlan, although this is somewhat by default because it is one of the few guides that covers the whole country in depth. Most guides either lump Lithuania, Latvia, and Estonia together or focus only on Vilnius. Unfortunately, the Bradt guide is getting a bit out of date, with the current edition published in 2008. It does, however, provide an unparalleled level of detail about areas off the main tourist trail, which can be quite valuable.

The In Your Pocket guides, available for the major cities and tourist destinations of Lithuania, and updated fairly frequently, are also very useful, although the inclusion of many ads can call into question the objectivity of some reviews. These can be purchased at various places, including the tourism offices, and are complimentary at some hotels. The guides are also available for free downloading or viewing at www.inyourpocket.com.

Souvenirs

There are plenty of opportunities to find souvenirs in Lithuania. In Vilnius, Pilies gatvė and Didžioji gatvė in particular are chock full of souvenir shops and street vendors. Note that prices at street vendors are negotiable to a certain extent should you want to try haggling.

The most classic souvenirs from Lithuania are those containing amber, especially jewelry. Amber trees, with small pieces of amber attached to wire fashioned into the shape of trees, are also common. Amber is quite plentiful and inexpensive; so much so, in fact, that there's little need to worry about the authenticity of amber that you're purchasing. I would, however, be more cautious with pieces of amber with insects inside them. Significant caution is warranted if that insect is wearing a tiny hat and holding a mini Lithuanian flag.

Souvenir Amber Trees

I always bring lots of chocolate and liquor back to the U.S. for gifts. The best place to shop for these is a grocery store. There are many different boxes of chocolate from which you can choose, partly because it is very customary in Lithuania to bring small gifts – chocolate, flowers, liquor, etc. – when visiting someone. I especially like the "Tūkstantmečio Lietuva" and "Gintaro Kelias" boxes – both made by Rūta (the company, not the woman). Karūna makes very good chocolate bars.

169

There are also plenty of small and souvenir size liquor bottles available for you to bring the taste of Lithuania back home. Keep in mind that you cannot bring liquor with an alcohol content that exceeds 70% on a plane to the U.S., and only up to 5 liters of liquor with alcohol content between 24% and 70%, as per TSA regulations. This limitation is separate from the customs limitations (discussed below).

You might be tempted to get one of the nesting dolls (**matryoshkas**) that are commonly on offer in the touristy areas. Feel free to pick one up, but just be aware that these are Russian, and Danny, this isn't Russia. (Is this Russia? This isn't Russia, is it? I didn't think so.) Don't go claiming you brought back a nice Lithuanian souvenir if this is all that you got.

Other classic souvenirs from Lithuania include linen products, handmade knits, and different forms of the uniquely Lithuanian crosses. Lithuanian cross-making is a very traditional craft, and Lithuanian crosses often incorporate symbols of nature, such as the sun. You may also be interested in honey, jams, teas, dried mushrooms and other food items that are generally of very high quality and relatively low price in Lithuania.

One type of souvenir that is extremely rare, surprisingly so for me, is t-shirts. This is true even in Palanga, the crazy beach town, which is just the type of place that would have tons of tacky t-shirt shops if it were in the U.S. After I expressed my surprise at the lack of t-shirt shops, my wife explained that Lithuanians (and Europeans in general) think that wearing shirts that show where you have been is pretty ridiculous. In line with that, people also don't wear shirts or any clothing that advertises what school they attended, as is also common in the

U.S. In general, Lithuanians shy away from being boastful, so they avoid these sorts of showy displays.

When bringing goods home from Lithuania, it is worth being mindful of the customs regulations for your country. Following is some advice regarding customs regulations in the U.S., but note that I am NOT providing legal advice, and you should look into these matters for yourself if you are concerned.

For the U.S., travelers coming from Lithuania will have a duty exemption on up to $800 worth of goods, although some goods like alcohol and tobacco have separate limitations. Up to one liter of alcohol may be brought into the U.S. duty-free. It is a common misperception that this alcohol limit means that no more than one liter may be brought back. This is not the case, and these limitations simply mean that duty will have to be paid on amounts greater than the limitations. Fortunately, George Costanza was basically right when he said "Duty's nothing – it's like sales tax!" The rate of duty is only 3%, meaning that in practice customs agents are unlikely to want to go through the paperwork for miniscule sums of duty. If you bring a reasonable amount of alcohol for personal use and gifts, go ahead and declare it, and you will probably just be waved through. Even if you do have to pay duty, it's not all that much.

One other matter that might trip you up in customs is that on the questionnaire, there is a question about whether you have things like seeds, vegetables, fruits, or *food*. It is fairly nonsensical to include the catch-all term "food," and I note that the automated kiosks for Global Entry travelers do not reference "food." After having compliantly checked "yes" for years, only to have the screeners roll their eyes at me, I have been told by a customs agent that they do not consider chocolate or candy to be "food."

When it comes to Canada, I have read that the country has extremely onerous duty on alcohol importation – something like 100% of the value above the exemptions, which for alcohol is 1.14 liters. If you are returning to Canada, I would advise investigating your options further.

Concluding Remarks

I hope you've enjoyed learning about Lithuania and that I've provided you with advice and guidance that you will find useful. I know that Lithuania is not on the top of most people's lists of dream vacations, but I think you'll agree that touring the country, meeting its people, and experiencing its culture is a valuable and enjoyable endeavor. There's always plenty of fun and delicious food waiting for you in Lithuania. I hope to see you in a Vilnius café soon!

If you are interested in learning even more about Lithuania, Part IV will provide you with a brief but comprehensive history of the country.

Part IV

History of Lithuania

Introduction

Lithuania has had a long and difficult history, but has proved remarkably resilient for a small nation in a precarious location in Europe. Its political history may best be characterized as a series of rises, falls, and rises again. The country held its millennial celebration in 2009, marking 1000 years since the first known mention of Lithuania in a text.[21] It is worth noting that the mention of Lithuania was in the context of pagans killing a missionary monk, which seems symbolic of much of the nation's history after such event. For much of the 10th through 15th centuries, Lithuanians fought to withstand Christian crusaders, as much (if not more) for protecting their territory as for religious reasons.

As with almost all other European countries, the borders of Lithuania have varied greatly over the years. At its largest, during the 15th century, Lithuania controlled the most expansive territory in all of Europe, including most of present-day Lithuania, Belarus, Ukraine and portions of Western Russia. On the other extreme, Lithuania has been absorbed into conquering empires numerous times, losing all status as an independent entity.

The tribes that came to be known as Lithuanians primarily inhabited the central and eastern regions of Lithuania prior to the consolidation of the state. The western (coastal) region of Lithuania was inhabited by a Baltic tribe called Curonians (**Kuršiai**), which were eventually assimilated into other groups. Another

---

[21] The following passage appeared in the Quedlinburg Annals (a German source of the 11th Century), dated 1009: "St. Bruno, an archbishop and monk, who was called Boniface, was struck in the head by Pagans during the 11th year of this conversion at the Rus and Lithuanian border, and along with 18 of his followers, entered heaven on March 9th."

Baltic tribe in the coastal regions, Prussians, was overtaken by invading Germans, and went out of existence as a distinct people. Much of the northwestern region of Lithuania was (and is) inhabited by Žemaitijans (once known as Samogitians).

Žemaitijans are a special case to consider: The region of Žemaitija was the subject of continuous fighting during the Middle Ages. During some periods, it was an independent entity, and during others, it was repeatedly traded back and forth between Lithuania and the Brothers of the Sword and Teutonic Knights in Livonia, with many rebellions by Žemaitijans also occurring. To this day, Žemaitijans retain the most distinct identity among the people considered ethnic Lithuanians.

Early History

Northeastern Europe near the Baltic Sea began to have some human inhabitants shortly after the glaciers receded in the period around 17000 to 15000 BC, and archaeological evidence suggests that the first permanent inhabitants settled around 9000 BC. During the period of approximately 3000 to 2500 BC, the first Indo-Europeans arrived in the area. These new arrivals mixed with the existing population, and eventually developed multiple distinct linguistic lines, resulting in what are known as the Baltic tribes.

During the last two millennia BC, with the introductions of bronze and iron, the Baltic tribes transitioned to living primarily in fixed settlements sustained by agricultural production. Many of these settlements included hillforts for communal protection, and by the first millennium AD many of these hillforts had become castles of the local lords.

The Balts were fairly isolated from the civilizations of Western Europe through the first millennium AD, although Western Europeans knew of the region's amber, which arrived through trade. The Balts had the most contact with Slavs, who moved into the areas inhabited by the western Balts in the 5th to 8th centuries AD, and with the Norse, who occasionally raided the coastal areas of the Curonians and Prussians. The Curonians, in turn, are known to have raided coastal Scandinavia.

During the later centuries of the first millennium AD, the most distinct characteristic of the Balts leading to their isolation from Western Europe was their paganism. Over time, many of the Balts' Slavic neighbors, particularly Poland in the West and Kievan Rus in the East, adopted Christianity. Shortly thereafter, many of the Scandinavians along the Baltic Sea also converted to Christianity. This situation as a pagan people surrounded by expansionist Christian rulers would play a central role in shaping the course of Lithuanian history for centuries.

10th through Mid-14thth Centuries: Formation of Lithuania/ Defense against Christian Crusaders

Much of Lithuania's recorded political history has been defined by its stance against foreign pressures. In the 10th through 14th centuries, Christianity (and the invaders who brought Christianity) spread throughout Scandinavia, Russia, Poland, Prussia and the lands along the northeastern Baltic Sea. Lithuanians, while not unified, stood out as one group that generally resisted this advance.

In response to the threat posed by the Order of the Knights of the Sword (German crusaders) coming from neighboring Livonia (present day Estonia and Latvia), Lithuanians began more formally uniting in common defense. One of the manifestations of this united front was a crushing defeat of the Order of the Brothers of the Sword by Žemaitijans led by Prince Vykintas in 1236 at the Battle of Saulė. This defeat led to the remaining Sword Brothers being folded into the Teutonic Order and ceasing to exist as a separate order.

During this period, and likely partly in response to the unification of Livonia and neighboring Prussian lands under the Teutonic Knights, Mindaugas emerged as a ruler of the unified Lithuanian lands around 1245. In order to consolidate his power, against both internal and external threats, Mindaugas negotiated to be crowned by the Pope as the King of Lithuania, which he was in 1253.[22] Although Mindaugas was baptized in 1251 and the church was formally established in Lithuania, there was little Christianization among the people of Lithuania for many years. In approximately 1261, as he planned renewed military actions against Livonia, Mindaugas renounced his conversion to Christianity (or revealed that he never accepted it in the first place).

Following Mindaugas' death in 1263, control of Lithuanian lands passed through several rulers until eventually Gediminas, considered one of Lithuania's most important rulers, took control in 1316. Gediminas ruled what had become known as the Grand Duchy of Lithuania, expanded its territory, and became

---

22 It should be noted that the matter of Mindaugas being referred to as the only "King" of Lithuania is based on his recognition as such by the Pope. Quite a few subsequent leaders of Lithuania were more powerful, ruled more people, controlled more land, and were referred to in Lithuania by words that could be translated as "King". These leaders are, however, generally referred to as "Grand Dukes," which is probably how they were recognized *outside* of Lithuania. It is somewhat curious to me, though probably based on the perspective of the eventual victors (Christians), that Lithuanians stand firm in the distinction that Mindaugas was the only King of Lithuania.

the patriarch of what is often referred to as the Gediminid Dynasty. In a repeat of Mindaugas' action, in 1323, Gediminas apparently sent a message to the Pope indicating his desire to be baptized, but when the papal envoy arrived in Vilnius in 1324, Gediminas refused to be baptized. In another twist, nearing his death in 1341, Gediminas invited Franciscan friars from Bohemia to baptize him, but they were killed somewhere along the way.

Within a few years of the death of Gediminas, one of his sons, Algirdas, took control of Lithuania, with another of Gediminas' sons, Kęstutis, playing a strong supporting role. Algirdas greatly expanded Lithuanian-controlled lands during the early part of his reign. Both Algirdas and Kęstutis offered at various times to convert to Christianity but, yet again, these plans fell through.

Late 14th through Late 18th Centuries: Unions with Poland/ Christianization/ Height of Power and Decline

After Algirdas' death in 1377, his son Jogaila came into conflict with Kęstutis and Kęstutis' son Vytautas (who became known as Vytautas the Great). After a period of conflict, during which Kęstutis died – likely murdered – in captivity, Vytautas and Jogaila eventually reconciled. Jogaila became King of Poland through marriage to Jadwiga (Lith.: Jadvyga), uniting the Kingdom of Poland and the Grand Duchy of Lithuania in a personal union. Vytautas eventually became Grand Duke of Lithuania – technically subservient to the King of Poland, but in reality a powerful sovereign in his own right. Members of the Jagiellonian dynasty controlled Poland until 1572, and ruled other Central and Eastern European lands throughout that time period.

Jogaila and Vytautas were both baptized as Catholics in 1386, which led to the widespread Christianization of Lithuania. The choice of Catholicism by Vytautas (instead of Orthodox Christianity) was an important and deliberate one, because it signified Lithuania's interest in strengthening ties with Western powers, instead of its Eastern neighbors. There appear to have been flirtations with the possibility of conversion to Orthodox Christianity, as a large portion of the Slavic peoples within the Grand Duchy of Lithuania were Orthodox. The Catholicism of the Polish-Lithuanian union would ultimately lead to significant conflict with the Orthodox Ruthenians (the Eastern Slavs) and Muscovites. The conversion of Lithuania did, however, provide a credible reason for other European powers to reduce their support for the Teutonic Order in its conflicts with Lithuania, as the Order had traditionally used Lithuania's paganism as a justification for its territorial ambitions in the region. Also, Christianization and union with Poland greatly expanded the influence of Western civilization in Lithuania, leading to an unprecedented period of cultural and economic growth in the 15th and 16th centuries.

Vytautas greatly expanded the territories of Lithuania through wars against the Golden Horde (the Mongols invading from the East) and Muscovy. Lithuania is, in fact, viewed as having played a vital role in stopping the advance of the Golden Horde into Europe. Also, in one of the most significant battles of the Middle Ages, Vytautas led his army, along with troops led by Jogaila, to victory against the Teutonic Order in the Battle of Grünwald (Lith.: **Žalgiris**, also known as the Battle of Tannenburg) on July 15, 1410. This battle, which resulted from a rebellion in Žemaitija and the subsequent incursion by the Teutonic Knights, was a resounding defeat for the Order. The defeat likely precipitated the Order's eventual dissolution, and is a celebrated event in Lithuanian history.

The union of Poland and Lithuania continued in an uneven but generally strong fashion throughout the 15th and 16th centuries. The culture and economy of Lithuania were able to flourish, especially in Vilnius. The Jesuit Academy of Vilnius (later renamed Vilnius University) was founded in 1579, and became one of the leading academic centers in Central and Eastern Europe. Rulers throughout this period encouraged trade by granting privileges to many groups, including Jews, who began to settle in Lithuanian cities in larger numbers. The economy of Lithuania, however, remained primarily reliant on agriculture, timber, and other raw materials. Because of the country's lack of ports and various regulations that favored wealthy landowners over merchants, relatively little wealth was generated from trade and other merchant activities. Throughout the period, a system of serfdom grew as smaller landowners and leaseholders lost their lands.

The union of the two countries was particularly important to Lithuania as a strong defensive alliance against the growing threat posed by Russia/Muscovy. Lithuania fought a series of wars with Russia during the period from 1492-1570, and in 1569 a weakened Lithuania agreed to the Union of Lublin with the Kingdom of Poland, creating the Commonwealth of the Two Nations. This Commonwealth was a joint state, but Poland was clearly the dominant partner. The new state had one ruler and assembly, with unified customs regulations and foreign policy. Lithuania remained a Grand Duchy within the Commonwealth and retained control over administration within its territory (including legislation), its treasury, army, and some other aspects of governmental affairs.

After the death of Sigismund Augustus, the last of the Jagiellonian dynasty, in 1572, the titles of King of Poland and Grand Duke of Lithuania became elected positions (and would be held by the same person). Unfortunately, the governance structure of the Commonwealth was flawed and very difficult to reform, and the country was further hampered by self-interested nobles who, in the later years of the Commonwealth, were often corrupted by foreign influence. Due to near constant wars, multiple famines and plagues, and economic recessions in Europe, the Commonwealth experienced a period of decline in its economic and military strength during the 17th century and early 18th century that would eventually result in its demise in the late 18th century.

During the 17th and 18th centuries, Lithuania and Poland were repeatedly caught in the middle of wars involving Sweden and Russia. After some Lithuanian nobles signed a treaty with Sweden in 1655, making Lithuania a Swedish protectorate, a conflict between Poles and Lithuanians on one side and Sweden and its Lithuanian allies on the other ravaged the country. Coupled with plagues that occurred during the same period, Lithuania lost nearly half of its population. Lithuania was also a battleground between Sweden and Russia during the Northern War of 1700-1721.

During the period of the Commonwealth of the Two Nations, the union's lands continued to include most of what is today Poland, Lithuania, Belarus and Ukraine. The nobility of the joint state leaned heavily toward Polish culture and language. The affairs of the state were generally conducted in Polish, and many Poles settled in and around Vilnius, resulting in Lithuanians being a small minority of the city's population.

This period also witnessed a substantial increase in the Jewish population throughout Lithuania, following the gradual immigration of Jews after Vytautas' invitations to Trakai in the late 14th century. By the middle of the 18th century, Lithuania had the highest density of Jews in the entire world. Vilnius became known as the "Jerusalem of the North" or the "Jerusalem of Europe" as it developed into an extremely important religious and cultural center, with a particular emphasis on Orthodox Judaism and opposition to Hasidism. The "Gaon of Vilna" ("Genius of Vilnius") was a famous rabbi who became a leader of the religious community and a foremost authority on Talmudic studies.

Late 18th through Early 20th Centuries: Incorporation into the Russian Empire and Emergence of an Ethno-political Movement

After a period of decline, the Commonwealth was divided among Russia, Prussia and Austria in a series of "partitions" between 1772 and 1795. During this period, in an attempt to make reforms that would stave off its decline, the Republic passed the first constitution in Europe in 1791 (second in the world after the U.S. Constitution). By 1795, Russia had annexed essentially all of what is now Central and Eastern Lithuania, as well as the former Lithuanian lands in the East (Belarus and Ukraine). Prussia gained control of Lithuania's coastal region (known as Lithuania Minor) and Suvalkija (southwestern region).

Tsarist rule was relatively steady until Napoleon's invasion in 1812, when Napoleon's army passed through Lithuania. Lithuania was briefly free from Russian rule, and began reorganizing into another union with Poland. After Napoleon's defeat and the Congress of Vienna in 1815, Lithuanian lands were returned to Russia, with the Suvalkija region being transferred to the Kingdom of Poland (also known as Congress Poland) (and eventually reintegrated into the Russian Empire during the 19th century).

After the reincorporation of Lithuanian lands into the Russian Empire, Russia imposed a series of restrictions on the region in order to suppress pro-independence movements. Russia put down an uprising in 1831, which had spread throughout Lithuania (especially Žemaitija). Vilnius University was closed in 1832, a policy of Russification (and de-Polonisation) was pursued, and the Russian legal system was established in the region (which was referred to as the "North-Western District"). Many Russians settled in Vilnius as Poles and others left.

In 1863, following the problematic abolition of serfdom in 1861, another peasant uprising began in Lithuania, again most strongly pursued in Žemaitija. Russia again quelled this rebellion, and imposed even harsher oppression in Lithuanian lands, accelerating its Russification policy, especially in education and public administration. Publication of books in Lithuanian or Polish, along with use of the Latin alphabet, was banned. Famously, **knygnešiai** (book smugglers) brought Lithuanian books published in Lithuania Minor (which was under the control of Prussia) into Russian-controlled Lithuania. Lithuanians in Lithuania Minor played an important role in the maintenance and revival of the national identity during the period of the worst Russian oppression.

Jews also suffered oppressions under Russian rule, particularly through codified attempts to assimilate Jews into Russian society, but Vilnius remained an important Jewish religious and cultural center. Institutions and publishing houses in Vilnius played strong roles in the Jewish Enlightenment of the late 19th century and the Zionist movement. It is estimated that Jews may have accounted for the majority of the Vilnius population at the end of the 19th century.

The first significant wave of emigration from Lithuania also took place in the late 19th century. Many of these emigrants went to the U.S.[23]

Political parties and cultural societies developed and matured in Lithuania during the late 19th century, and began to slowly pressure the Russian government into allowing greater freedoms. In 1904, the ban on publishing in the Lithuanian language was lifted, although publications remained censored. In 1905, simultaneously with a revolutionary movement occurring in Russia, Lithuanians took steps to declare their independence and establish an autonomous government. While little real progress was made, and Russia firmly squashed the revolution, this episode laid the groundwork for the political organization of Lithuania that would be necessary to successfully gain independence a little over a decade later.

During this period and after, the issue of what sort of state should be formed was vigorously debated and contested. Some viewed Lithuania's future as intertwined with Poland, and advocated a return to union with that country. Others imagined Lithuania as the Grand Duchy, with the lands of Lithuania and

---

[23] My wife's grandmother was born in the U.S., but returned to Lithuania with her parents. Unfortunately, the money that the family had earned in the U.S. was quickly confiscated by officials of tsarist Russia. My wife remembers her grandmother having a rather irrational fear of acquiring any material possessions, because she feared that they would be taken away.

Belorussia joined together. The newest concept of Lithuania, and the one that ultimately prevailed, was a country based primarily on the regions inhabited by ethnic Lithuanians. Lithuanians began to develop an ethno-political consciousness in place of the previously dominant political aspirations of the gentry. A Lithuanian movement based on shared language and religion began to grow, especially among peasants.

1915-1940: World War I and Independence

Germany invaded the Lithuanian region of the Russian Empire in 1915. As with much of Eastern Europe, the war was devastating to Lithuania. The city of Šiauliai and many smaller towns and villages were almost completely destroyed.

While still occupied by Germany, the Council of Lithuania, headed by Jonas Basanavičius, declared Lithuanian independence on February 16, 1918. Germany was supportive of Lithuania's independence, although Germany conceived of Lithuania as a dependent satellite state. At the time, peace negotiations between Soviet Russia and Germany had just broken down, and Germany had resumed military hostilities against Russia on February 15. On March 3, 1918, Russia and the Central Powers agreed to end their war and signed the Treaty of Brest-Litovsk, in which Russia ceded portions of its former empire. After the treaty, Germany continued to occupy Lithuania and exercise significant control over it. At Germany's urging, the Council of Lithuania declared a constitutional monarchy in July of 1918 and even elected (but never crowned) a German king, Duke Wilhelm von Urach-Württemberg, designating him Mindaugas II.

After the defeat of Germany in the fall of 1918, the Council of Lithuania took control of the country and established a national government. The act establishing the constitutional monarchy and the election of the king were revoked in November of 1918.The country was founded in accordance with the emerging concept of self-determination, and sought to be a nation-state that united the territories of ethnic Lithuanians but that recognized the rights of minorities.

Conditions in Lithuania were chaotic following the formal end of the war. Lithuania sought to quickly mobilize an army to defend against the threat of Soviet Russia. Germany assisted Lithuania's military efforts to some extent by paying reparations, keeping troops stationed in Lithuania, and sending a volunteer German brigade, while Lithuania raised a small army of its own. The Red Army quickly took over Vilnius and the surrounding area after the Lithuanian government retreated and Lithuanian communists had established a revolutionary government in Vilnius.

Soviet forces (including some communist Lithuanians) battled German and Lithuanian forces back and forth in Lithuania. Lithuanian forces fought the Soviets throughout 1919, continuing to drive them farther back. At the same time, Polish troops had been driving back the Soviets in Poland and Southern Lithuania, trading control of Vilnius with the Soviets.

Lithuanian territory, and its very existence as an independent state, was threatened not only by the Soviets, but also by the Polish forces and a rogue military group called the Bermondtists. Polish units engaged Lithuanian troops multiple times in Southern Lithuania, and a coup was planned by Polish agents in an attempt to overthrow the Lithuanian government. In the northern part of the country, Lithuanian troops had to contend with soldiers led by Pavel Bermondt (the Bermondtists), comprised of White Russians and remnants of German divisions. The Bermondtists rampaged throughout Latvia and Northern Lithuania, but ultimately were defeated in November of 1919.

In July of 1920, Soviet Russia and Lithuania concluded a treaty recognizing the territory of Lithuania, including Vilnius, as an independent country. However, in October of 1920, Polish troops seized Vilnius and the Suvalkija region – areas of mixed Lithuanian and Polish populations. The Lithuanian government established a temporary capital in Kaunas. Vilnius was officially annexed by Poland in 1923.

In its own turn at territorial aggression, Lithuania annexed the important port city of Memel (Klaipėda) and the region known as Lithuania Minor in 1923. Memel had been taken from the German Empire according to the Treaty of Versailles and had become a mandate of the League of Nations. The city was under French administration, including a garrison of French troops, until its fate could be decided – likely to be turned into a free city similar to nearby Danzig (Gdansk). Lithuania fomented an uprising of the local Lithuanian population, which claimed its right of self-determination, and the city was officially transferred to Lithuania without any meaningful objection from the League of Nations.

During the hectic first year of its existence, Lithuania was governed by the Lithuanian Council, and in April of 1919, Antanas Smetona became the first President. The first parliament, the Foundation Seimas, declared Lithuania a parliamentary republic in 1920, but this only lasted until 1926, when Antanas Smetona returned to power in a coup. Smetona revised the constitution to vest significant authority in the President, and remained in power until the eve of WWII.

During its brief independence, Lithuania struggled diligently to modernize and westernize, pursuing free market economics and private ownership of property, and it was able to achieve a measure of economic advancement. However, the country's economy remained primarily agricultural. Possession of Klaipėda proved very advantageous, because much of the country's trade flowed through it and the city contained a large portion of the country's industrial facilities. During the period of independence, Jewish businesses in Lithuania played a very important role in the Lithuanian economy. Also during this period, the second significant wave of emigration to the West, including the U.S., occurred.

World War II

As with most of Europe, World War II represents a very dark period in Lithuania's history. Lithuania suffered through an initial Soviet occupation, a German occupation, and a subsequent re-occupation by the Soviets until 1991, experiencing terrible atrocities at the hands of these occupiers.

Leading up to the war, Lithuania was precariously positioned between an increasingly strong and aggressive Germany and a USSR that retained territorial ambitions in the Baltic countries. As tensions mounted in 1939, the USSR and Germany secretly signed a non-aggression pact on August 23, 1939. The now notorious Molotov-Ribbentrop Pact[24] included a secret protocol that divided Northern and Eastern Europe into Soviet and German "spheres of influence" and recognized each country's right to annex those territories. The Pact placed Lithuania with-

---

[24] Officially, "The Treaty of Non-Aggression between Germany and the Soviet Union".

in the German sphere of influence, although a later agreement[25] signed shortly after the first allocated most of Lithuania to the Soviet sphere of influence.

After increasingly aggressive ultimatums by the Soviet Union demanding that Lithuania allow Red Army military bases in its territory, the Soviet Union demanded the resignation of the Lithuanian parliament and orchestrated the election of pro-Soviet members.[26] Concurrently, the Red Army moved into Lithuania on June 15, 1940, taking control of the country. A newly-formed government declared Lithuania a Soviet Socialist Republic and officially recognized its incorporation into the USSR. Soviets quickly began a campaign of Sovietization in occupied Lithuania, including nationalization of property and enterprises, collectivization of agricultural production, arrests, mass deportations and murders. As had occurred in Soviet Russia, the intelligentsia was particularly targeted for arrest and deportations to Siberia.[27]

The brutal Sovietization of Lithuania came to a halt when Germany invaded the Soviet Union in June of 1941, moving into Lithuania and the other Baltic countries. Due to the oppression experienced under Soviet rule, many Lithuanians initially viewed the Germans as liberators and some Lithuanians

---

[25] The German–Soviet Treaty of Friendship, Cooperation and Demarcation, signed on September 28, 1939.

[26] This event represents one of the great divides between the Soviet/Russian narrative and the narrative recognized by most of the rest of the world regarding the annexation of Lithuania. The Russian narrative is that the incorporation of Lithuania was a voluntary act conducted by an elected government, whereas most of the rest of the world views it as a hostile takeover. In Lithuania, the period of Soviet control is viewed as an illegal occupation, thus the "independence" declared in 1990 was technically a re-establishment of *de facto* independence but that Lithuania had continued to be legally independent since 1918.

[27] Many of my wife's relatives were deported to Siberia and this period is considered very sad for her family.

participated in rising up against the Soviets and took retribution against communists, including a number of massacres. Lithuanians also set up a new government, which they hoped could operate semi-autonomously from Germany.

Unfortunately, the Nazis intended to transform Lithuania by eliminating the "undesirable elements" of the population, which meant for the most part the Jewish population. As elsewhere in Europe, the Nazis used propaganda targeted against Jews to bolster local support for their agenda. Specific to Lithuania and the Baltic countries was the Nazi message that Jews were collaborators with the Soviets. Leveraging this negative message and long-standing anti-Semitism, the Nazis did receive some support from Lithuanian police units, although the exact extent of Lithuanian support for mass killing of Jews remains a point of contention.

Unlike in many other occupied countries, the Nazis moved extremely quickly with the genocide of Lithuanian Jews in the early months of occupation. The most notable mass executions occurred at the Ninth Fort outside of Kaunas and in the forest of Paneriai, near Vilnius. Following the initial mass executions of 1941, ghettos were established in Vilnius, Kaunas, Šiauliai, and Švenčionys, confining the Jews who had survived the initial killings. From the middle of 1943 to the middle of 1944, most of the Jews remaining in the ghettos were either transferred to concentration camps or killed in the ghettos.

The Nazi occupation was absolutely devastating to the Lithuanian Jewish population. The percentage of the Jewish population killed in Lithuania was the highest of any country, at an estimated 94-97% of the Jewish population. In total, approximately 190,000 to 220,000 Jews were killed in Lithuania, with an astonishing estimated 136,000 of those being killed in the first six months of Nazi occupation.

The ethnic Lithuanian population, while generally faring far better than the Jewish population, also suffered worsening treatment under Nazi occupation. Collaborators were tolerated by the Nazi regime, but others faced arrest, deportation to forced labor camps, or being sent to concentration camps for resisting cooperation. The Nazi plan was to ultimately deport or kill most of the ethnic Lithuanian population, and assimilate those deemed desirable with a German population that would be brought into the region.

During the Nazi occupation, several groups of partisans participated in anti-Nazi fighting, most notably a Polish resistance group in the Vilnius region, Soviet partisan forces, and some Jewish partisan fighters.

1944-1991: Soviet Occupation

As the tide of the war turned, the Soviets returned to Lithuania in the summer of 1944 as the Red Army pushed German forces back toward Germany. Soviet forces also encountered and fought against Polish forces around Vilnius as they took that city in early July. Soviet forces took Kaunas in early August and encountered heavy resistance at the German front line at Šiauliai, resulting again in that city's near total destruction. The Red Army renewed its efforts against Germans in Žemaitija in October of 1944, then moved toward Klaipėda, taking the city in January of 1945 and completing the Soviet takeover of Lithuania.

The USSR reconstituted the Lithuanian Soviet Socialist Republic, which included the city of Vilnius as its capital. Mass arrests of the educated class, civil administrators, police, members of the military and others were undertaken by the Soviets, and Russian administrators flowed into the country. The Soviets quickly reintroduced Sovietization policies, commencing mass deportations of Lithuanians to Siberia and terrorizing the population with the secret police forces of the NKVD (the precursor to the KGB). Over 130,000 Lithuanians were deported to Siberia during Stalin's time in power. The Soviet Union also initiated a military draft of Lithuanians, with tens of thousands of Lithuanians being forced into the Red Army during the early years of Soviet occupation.[28]

Approximately 140,000 ethnic German residents of the Klaipėda region and approximately 200,000 ethnic Poles from the Vilnius region left the country to escape the Soviets. Tens of thousands of Lithuanians, including a sizable portion of the most educated and best trained part of the population who would have been most targeted by the Soviets, also fled the country and ended up in Displaced Persons camps in Germany after the war. Most of these Lithuanians would eventually emigrate to other countries, especially the U.S., Canada, the UK and Australia, once it became apparent that return to a free Lithuania was not an option.

In the early years following the reoccupation of Lithuania by the USSR, hopes remained high among Lithuanians that the West would support their attempts to reestablish independence. An organized armed resistance movement known as the Forest Brothers, so named due to their use of the forests for hiding, developed to fight the Soviets. An estimated 100,000 Lithuanians took part in armed resistance during the period of 1944 to

---

[28] My wife's grandfather spent about 10 months hiding in a bunker to avoid being drafted into the Soviet army.

1951. The partisan resistance was eventually worn down, particularly due to infiltration by Soviet agents, and armed conflict lasted until 1953 – one of the longest armed resistances to Soviet occupation in Europe.

Lithuania followed a similar course as the rest of the Soviet republics, with control highly centralized in Moscow. During the Stalin era, Lithuanian society was dramatically transformed through mass deportations, suppression of national identity and religion, nationalization of property, and collectivization of industry and agriculture. The KGB was a constant threat to the freedom of Lithuanians, and it carried out a campaign of terror against the populace. Russians dominated governmental positions throughout Lithuania.

Starting in the mid-1950s, during the Khrushchev era, there was a slight relaxation of Moscow's firm grip on Lithuania. Governmental positions opened up to more Lithuanians, and there was slightly more tolerance of the Lithuanian language and culture, at least unofficially. However, the country continued to suffer significantly under communism and rule from Moscow. Also during this period, some Lithuanians who had been deported to Siberia began to return to Lithuania, where they often found re-integration to be a difficult task.

Soviet control of Lithuania changed many aspects of Lithuanians' everyday lives. The familiar system of communist Soviet life played out in Lithuania as it did in the rest of the Soviet Union. Employment was generally guaranteed, and apartments and cars were allocated out to families, with members of the Communist Party receiving the best available. Service in the Soviet military was compulsory for males. Soviet propaganda was propagated in schools. Press was controlled by the government and only published approved stories. Rampant industrialization with little concern for pollution control led to widespread environmental damage. Lithuania also became substantially more urbanized during the middle decades of Soviet occupation along with this industrialization.

Quality goods were scarce, and waiting for a particular desired good was common. The collectivization of agriculture generally led to a decline in agricultural productivity and the state industries produced low quality products. Lithuanians did, however, achieve significant agricultural productivity on the small private plots of land (**sodai**) that they were allowed to farm for personal purposes.

Significant numbers of Russian workers came to Lithuania during Soviet times, as the USSR established the industrial base of the country. Interestingly, some of the largest projects in Lithuania were related to power production, most notably the recently-closed Ignalina Nuclear Power Plant and the Mažeikiai oil refinery, as well as the Kaunas hydro-electric plant (with the creation of the Kauno Marios (a large reservoir called the "Kaunas Sea")) and the power plant at Elektrėnai.[29] The Soviets also established a significant manufacturing sector in Lithuania.

The slight liberalization that began in the Khrushchev era lasted through the 1960s, but was eventually reversed in the late 1960s. The country continued to stagnate under Soviet rule, but there was an increase in open opposition to the oppression by the Soviets. In a notable display of protest, a student named Romas Kalanta set himself on fire in Kaunas in 1972, an act which led to student protests and is today commemorated with

---

[29] This town was established during Soviet times and was creatively named essentially "Electric Town" – its coat of arms has two lightning bolts on it.

a statue on Laisves alėja (Freedom Street) in that city. Other forms of opposition were evidenced by groups supporting human rights, environmental movements, cultural activities and pursuing freedom to practice Catholicism.

The early 1980s saw a return of significant oppression of opposition elements in Lithuania. Soviets cracked down on various groups that had been allowed to operate underground during the 1970s and early 1980s. Fortunately, this period was short-lived, with Gorbachev implementing reforms in the mid- to late-1980s that would dramatically alter the political scene in Lithuania.

As Gorbachev's policies of *glasnost* and *perestroika* began to be implemented throughout the Soviet Union, Lithuanian groups took the opportunity to increase their anti-Soviet activities. One of the first major events was a rally held in Vilnius in August of 1987 to commemorate the 48th anniversary of the Molotov-Ribbentrop Pact, part of the Lithuanian push for the USSR to acknowledge the illegality of its occupation based on the secret protocols with Germany in 1939.

In 1988, the Sąjūdis Reform Movement was established in Vilnius by a group of academic and cultural leaders, including its head, Prof. Vytautas Landsbergis. Sąjūdis played a critical role in organizing protests throughout Lithuania, as the movement toward greater autonomy and ultimately, freedom, gained momentum. Protests often involved traditional Lithuanian songs, and song festivals became important venues for massive demonstrations of national pride, leading to the term the Singing Revolution (a name used to refer to the movements in all of the Baltic countries).

Another gathering in Vilnius in August of 1988, again marking the anniversary of the Molotov-Ribbentrop Pact, drew as many as 150,000 participants, illustrating the increasingly widespread appeal of the movement. In October of 1988, Sąjūdis held a founding congress, which set out the demands of the people for full independence of Lithuania. At this time, Sąjūdis established itself as an actual opposition party to the Communist Party. In 1989, it won 36 out of 42 seats contested in Lithuania for the Congress of People's Deputies, the highest Soviet legislative body, created that year as part of Gorbachev's reforms and the first elections to be open to non-Communist Party candidates.

In August of 1989, on the occasion of the 50th anniversary of the Molotov-Ribbentrop Pact, an extraordinary display of unity among the people of the Baltic countries occurred. About 2 million people joined hands in a human chain from Vilnius, through Riga, to Tallinn, in what is known as the Baltic Way.

In 1990, Sąjūdis secured a majority of the seats in the Supreme Council of Lithuania and declared the independence of Lithuania on March 11, 1990. The Soviet Union refused to recognize the country's independence, and imposed an economic blockade against Lithuania, including cutting off almost all energy supplies. On January 13, 1991, Soviet troops moved to overthrow the Lithuanian government, and attempted to take over government buildings and the TV tower. Civilians massed around the tower and government buildings, and the ensuing clashes at the TV tower resulted in the deaths of fourteen Lithuanians.

In August of 1991, following a coup in Moscow, most countries formally recognized Lithuania's independence.[30] Lithuania joined the United Nations on September 17, 1991. The last Russian troops left Lithuania on August 31, 1993.

Interestingly, although Lithuania had many Russians in the country during Soviet times, it never ended up with a sizable permanently settled Russian population, with which Estonia and Latvia are now struggling. This is partly due to the fact that Lithuania had no single dominant city to which Russians would relocate, in contrast to Tallinn in Estonia and Riga in Latvia. In addition, it is thought that certain key Lithuanians in power in the Lithuanian SSR actually worked toward limiting the number of Russians that came to Lithuania. This has been quite a fortunate outcome for the country, as Russia has not interfered in Lithuania's internal affairs as much as it has in Estonia and Latvia.

1991-Present: Restored Independence

Lithuania emerged from the Soviet Union into a globalized world that had progressed in many ways much more than had the Soviet republics. The country had been fully-integrated into the Soviet economy, with relatively inefficient industries trading with other Soviet republics. Suddenly, the country was removed from that system and set out on its own. The people of Lithuania suffered tremendous hardships, including food and fuel shortages, rampant inflation, and massive unemployment (resulting from the closure of many unsustainable industries). Significant backlash against the economic reforms of the country emerged, and many members of the former Communist Party,

---

[30] The notable exception is Iceland, which had formally recognized Lithuania in February of 1991. Vilnius and Kaunas (and perhaps other cities) have streets named after Iceland to honor this.

refashioned as the Labor Party, were elected. Another significant wave of emigration occurred, as Lithuanians sought more opportunity abroad. Although the freedoms gained because of the country's independence and democratic reforms were favorable, the country desperately needed to experience economic growth in order to successfully transition to a stable, liberal democracy.

Fortunately, the country's political and economic reforms did begin to provide a platform for the establishment of a growing market economy. While many local industries were forced to close, foreign direct investment (especially from the Scandinavian countries) moved into the country to take advantage of the well-educated and relatively inexpensive workforce. Gradually, the economy recovered and began to grow, and by the 2000s it was growing at one of the fastest rates in Europe. The average income of Lithuanians has now increased dramatically, and the gap between per capita GDP in Lithuania and per capita GDP in Western Europe has decreased substantially.

Political reforms and the integration of Lithuania into the international community have progressed steadily. The Constitution established a unicameral system with a prime minister and president. Corruption, though still a problem, has been curtailed significantly. Elections have become competitive affairs, with multiple parties vying for control and coalition governments being commonplace. Lithuania joined the European Union and NATO in 2004.

The world economic crisis affected Lithuania to a great extent, with a sizable contraction in the country's GDP in 2009. The government has very aggressively instituted painful austerity measures, in an attempt to avoid a sovereign debt crisis. Fortunately, it appears that the country is emerging from economic stagnation and the worst of the crisis has passed.

Lithuania has survived many centuries of turmoil and is now emerging as an important member of the international community. Though many challenges still exist, the country has accomplished so much since Soviet occupation, and has significant potential for a long and prosperous future.

Photo Credits

Pictures are identified by their captions used in the book and listed in the order of appearance. Unless otherwise noted, photographs are copyrighted with All Rights Reserved by their respective authors and are used herein with express permission of each such author.

If marked "CC BY 2.0" below, the photo is subject to a Creative Commons Attribution 2.0 Generic (CC BY 2.0) license.

If marked "CC BY-SA 2.0" below, the photo is subject to a Creative Commons Attribution-ShareAlike 2.0 Generic license.

If marked "CC BY-SA 3.0" below, the photo is subject to a Creative Commons Attribution-ShareAlike 3.0 Unported license.

You can access the description of all of these licenses via http://creativecommons.org/licenses/.

Maps of Lithuania. Photos from CIA World Factbook

View of Vilnius Cathedral and Gedimino prospektas. Photo by Nahuel G. Rebollar; retrieved from Flickr; CC BY 2.0

Forest trail in a birch and pine forest near Trakai. Photo by Columbia J. Warren

Traditional sodybos in rural Lithuania. Photo by Kazys Mikalauskas

Bend of the Nemunas river in Dzūkija. Photo by Kazys Mikalauskas

Agritourism cottage at Samanis. Photo by Columbia J. Warren

Trakai Castle and Lake Galvė. Photo by Mindaugas Danys; retrieved from Flickr; CC BY 2.0.

Cute little hedgehog (ežiukas). Photo by Tomi Tapio; retrieved from Flickr; CC BY 2.0

Storks hunting. Photo by Vytasmil; retrieved from Flickr; CC BY 2.0.

Šakotis in the process of being made. Photo by Ugnė Lipeikaitė

Crowd celebrating a basketball victory in the Kaunas Town Hall Square. Photo by Kazys Mikalauskas

View over the Old Town of Vilnius. Photo by davehighbury; retrieved from Flickr; CC BY-SA 2.0

Financial district in Vilnius with the Europa Tower (the tallest building in the Baltic States) second from the left. Photo by Arroww; retrieved from Wikipedia; CC BY-SA 3.0

Vilnius, one of the greenest capitals in Europe. Photo by Chad Kainz; retrieved from Flickr; CC BY 2.0

View of Vilnius Cathedral from the side, showing the Chapel of Saint Casimir on the right. Photo by FaceMePLS; retrieved from Flickr; CC BY 2.0

Church of Saint Anne (left), Church of St. Francis of Assisi (middle), and 19th century bell tower (right). Photo by Šarūnas Burdulis; retrieved from Flickr; CC BY 2.0

Church of St. Casimir. Photo by philantrophde; retrieved from Flickr; CC BY 2.0

Gates of Dawn, with the icon of the Virgin Mary visible through the window. Photo by Alexandre Vialle; retrieved from Flickr; CC BY 2.0

202

Angel statue in Užupis. Photo by Colin Warren

Trakai Island Castle. Photo by Columbia J. Warren

Old Town of Kaunas and the confluence of the Nemunas and Neris rivers. Photo by Kazys Mikalauskas

Old Town of Kaunas. Photo by Kazys Mikalauskas

Memorial at the Kaunas Ninth Fort. Photo by Tadas Kuzminskas

Pažaislis Monastery. Photo by Kazys Mikalauskas

Inner courtyard in Klaipėda's Old Town. Photo by Nikater; retrieved from Wikipedia; CC BY-SA 2.0

Druskonis lake in Druskininkai. Photo by Vytasmil; retrieved from Flickr; CC BY 2.0

Pušynas Hotel - an example of interesting Soviet architecture. Photo by Columbia J. Warren

Seated Lenin (a rare position for Lenin sculptures), previously located in the center of Druskininkai. Photo by Columbia J. Warren

Sunset at Palanga Pier. Photo by Aurelijus Valeiša; retrieved from Flickr; CC BY 2.0

Magnificent Dunes of Curonian Spit. Photo by Ligita Leistromaitė

Hill of Crosses. Photo by Kyle Taylor; retrieved from Flickr; CC BY 2.0

Three Muses in front of the National Drama Theatre. Photo by Alistair Young; retrieved from Flickr; CC BY 2.0

Souvenir Amber Trees. Photo by Aušra Milano

ABOUT THE AUTHOR

Columbia J. Warren is a frequent traveler to Lithuania and lives in Ithaca, NY with his wife, Jūratė. The couple met at the University of Virginia while attending graduate school and were married in the summer of 2011 in Jūratė's hometown of Druskininkai. After working as a corporate attorney in Boston, Columbia is now a research administrator at Cornell University, where his wife is an Economics Professor. Columbia is an avid runner, having run five marathons – twice qualifying for the Boston Marathon. He also enjoys skiing, traveling, reading, and playing with his cat, Tobis.

Made in the USA
Lexington, KY
06 November 2013